malabar muslim cookery

Brought up in a large Moplah joint family, cooking came instinctively to Ummi Abdulla. Some sound practical training in cookery at the Madras Institute of Catering Technology and Applied Nutrition has given a scientific basis to her natural expertise. She lives in Madras and is currently in charge of a modest cottage industry to make pickles, jams and masala powders. Married to a senior publishing consultant, she has three children.

Cooking = kitchen + hungry family

serving = art + hungry family

cookbook = writing + kitchen + testing + hungry family

This book is dedicated to the common factor

malabar muslim cookery

Ummi Abdulla

Illustrations by
Anant Kulkarni

Orient BlackSwan

MALABAR MUSLIM COOKERY

ORIENT BLACKSWAN PRIVATE LIMITED

Registered Office
3-6-752 Himayatnagar, Hyderabad 500 029, Telangana, India
Email: centraloffice@orientblackswan.com

Other Offices
Bengaluru, Chennai, Guwahati, Hyderabad, Kolkata
Mumbai, New Delhi, Noida, Patna

First published 1981
First published in Disha Books by Orient Blackswan Pvt. Ltd. 1993
Reprinted 1999, 2005
Reissued 2009
Reprinted 2012, 2014, 2015, 2018, 2020, 2024

ISBN 978-81-250-1349-5

Typeset by
Fotocomp Systems
Mumbai

038570

Printed at
B.B. Press, Noida 201 301

Published by
Orient Blackswan Private Limited
3-6-752 Himayatnagar, Hyderabad 500 029, Telangana, India
Email: info@orientblackswan.com

CONTENTS

INTRODUCTION

The Malayalam-speaking Muslims of Kerala, more particularly of the northern part of the State called Malabar, are known as Moplahs. The word is supposed to be a variant of 'Mapillai' meaning bridegroom, or 'Maha Pillai', meaning a person held in esteem. It is an indication of the respect accorded to the Kerala Muslims at least originally. They were descended from Arab intermarriage with local Kerala women and of the Arab traders who came to trade and settled down. Later they proliferated with accretions to their ranks by conversion to Islam. The inhabitants of Kerala (literally, 'the land of coconuts') were orthodox, caste-bound Hindus but they were tolerant of rebellion from within their faith as well as of religions which came from outside. It is no paradox that Sri Adi Sankara was born in Kerala, that the first synagogue, church and mosque in India were established in Kerala with State assistance and the first elected Communist Ministry in the country came into being there.

Though the Moplahs are linguistically one with the rest of the population of Kerala, they have a certain sub-cultural individuality of their own which is reflected in their separate way of life. Their cuisine exudes special Moplah flavours, though it has a great deal in common with food élsewhere in Kerala in its excessive use of coconut and coconut oil, and in its dependence on rice as the staple item of food. The Arab influence is evident in some of the dishes like *Alisa*, a wholesome wheat and meat porridge, and stuffed chicken. The famous *biriyani* must have been brought from Samarkhand by the Moghuls and the indigenous Muslim rulers of Arcot and Mysore, though the Moplah variations are noteworthy. There is, however, a certain variety of dishes that is intrinsically Moplah and recognised as such by all Malayalis — the *pathiri* or rice chapati made in many different ways, the *Neichoru*, an exotic fried rice and the sweet *Mutta mala* or the 'egg-garland' made of the yolk of eggs without a trace of fat.

A large number of Moplah specialities are intended for festive occasions, and no introduction of Moplah cuisine would be complete without a brief account of these festivities. The most festive occasion, is of course, a wedding in the family. Though a simple contractual agreement like all Muslim weddings, the Nikah performed by the Kazi is preceded and followed by a great deal of feasting. *Neichoru* is normally served on *mailanchi* night, the eve of the wedding, when henna is applied on the bride's hands and feet. Biriyani is served on the wedding night. *Mutta mala* is traditionally served at the wedding in large porcelain plates with *Pinhanathapam*, forming artistic yellow and white designs. On the morning after the wedding, the groom and his friends are treated to a sumptuous festive breakfast of stuffed chicken and *pathiris*, a wide choice of curries, *puttus* with the long Kerala banana, *Kanji* or rice gruel and the ubiquitous *chai* or tea to which the Moplah is addicted. Moplah cuisine thrives during the holy month of Ramzan, when the religious fast from dawn to sunset is broken with water and dry dates. After the prayers, a rich meal of *pathiris* and meat and chicken is served, followed by a snack and a meal later to provide enough sustenance for the next day. Festivals ordained by tradition have their own Moplah specialities both sweet and savoury.

Everyday Moplah cuisine, though spicy and hot, consists of wholesome rather than rich variations of Moplah specialities. Plain rice accompanied by some form of fish is the most common, alternated by meat and chicken. In certain North Malabar households, the night meal is restricted to *pathiri* and *kanji*. The traditional Moplah breakfast is a hearty, filling meal of pancakes, egg curry or egg masala, or *puttu* and hot fish curry.

I have, in this work, attempted to include a large range of Moplah recipes to suit commonplace meals and special occasions. Traditional Moplah dishes have been discussed, keeping in mind, as far as possible, the limitations and conveniences of a modern kitchen. A few of the items are my own improvisations based on conventional modes. As far as I know this is the first book of its kind on Moplah cookery. I place it before the reader with some trepidation, knowing how easy it is to slip up on the innumerable details which are a vital part of any cook-book.

A word about some of the special vessels used in making certain items. *Puttus*, or steamed rice cakes, are made in a special cylindrical container attached to a narrow-necked vessel which, filled three quarters with water and boiled, lets out the steam which passes through the *puttu* in the cylindrical container. A perforated round lid at the bottom of the cylinder keeps the *puttu* flour intact. Traditionally, a hollow bamboo was attached to a mud pot to make up this contraption but today aluminium or steel units are available in the market. *Meen pathiris* or *adukurotis* were made in what are called 'bandu chembus' but they are basically idli-making vessels which would do just as well. The noodle-like *Mutta* mala is made by letting the egg-yolk drop through a hole in a wooden spoon consisting of a bamboo handle and at the broad end a hemispherical coconut shell with a hole in the centre. Any ladle with a suitable hole in the centre would do of course. Traditionally, baked items were made by pouring the mixture into any good vessel and heating it over coal or charcoal with the top of the vessel covered by a metal lid on which there would be live charcoal. This is of course primitive baking without moulds and so on. These items can be made just as well in any modern oven using either gas or electricity.

I cannot conclude without a word of thanks to Orient Longman, the publishers. My thanks are specially due to the Company's Chairman, Raja J. Rameshwar Rao, but for whose appreciative comments on Moplah cooking I would not have thought of this book at all. My thanks are also due to Usha Aroor and Vidya Hyderi who have patiently seen the manuscript and the book through all stages of writing.

This is my first book and it has taken me three years to compile. I hope the English readers will find it useful. I would consider my efforts recompensed if at least some of the traditional Moplah recipes find a permanent place on the Indian menu.

Ummi Abdulla
March 1981

RICE AND WHOLE WHEAT FARE

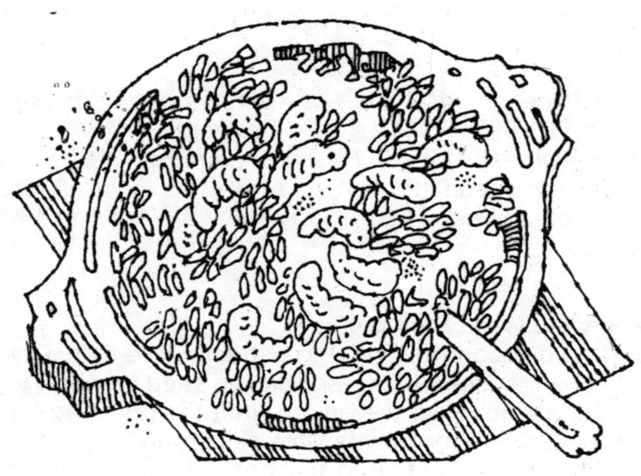

1. Neichoru

(Ghee Rice)

Pulao rice	*500 gm.*	*Cardamom*	*2 pods*
Onions (large)	*2*	*Ghee*	*4 tbsp.*
Cloves	*2*	*Salt*	*to taste*
Cinnamon	*4 cm. piece*		

Clean, wash and drain the rice. Slice the onion. Heat the ghee. Add the onion, cinnamon, cloves and cardamom. Fry till the onion is transparent. Add the rice and fry for 3 - 4 minutes. Add boiling water (double the quantity of rice) and salt. Cook till the rice is soft and the water is absorbed. Serve hot with mutton or chicken curry.

2. Thenga Choru
(Coconut Rice)

Boiled rice	*400 gm.*	*Cinnamon*	*4 cm. piece*
Coconut	*½*	*Cloves*	*3*
Onion (large)	*1*	*Cardamoms*	*2*
Coriander seeds	*2 tsp.*	*Ghee*	*2 tbsp.*
Turmeric powder	*1 tsp.*	*Salt*	*to taste.*
Aniseed	*2 tsp.*		

Clean and wash the rice.
Grate the coconut. Grind it to extract ½ litre milk. Grind the coriander seeds, turmeric and aniseed together to a smooth paste. Slice the onion. Heat the ghee, add the onion, cardamom, cloves and cinnamon. Fry till the onion is transparent. Add the ground masala and stir well. Pour in the coconut milk, ½ litre water and salt to taste. When the coconut milk boils add the washed rice. If the milk is not sufficient to cook the rice add some more hot water. Cook till the rice is done and the moisture absorbed. Serve hot with mutton curry.

3. Birinji
(Turmeric Rice)

Boiled rice	*400 gm.*	*Ghee or oil*	*2 tbsp.*
Onion (large)	*1*	*Turmeric powder*	*1 tsp.*
Coriander seeds	*2 tsp.*	*Salt*	*to taste*
Aniseed	*2 tsp.*		

Grind the coriander seeds, aniseed and turmeric powder to a smooth paste. Slice the onion. Heat the ghee and fry the onion till lightly browned. Add sufficient water to cook the rice.

Add the ground masala mixed with a little water and stir. Add salt and let the water boil. Clean and wash the rice, and add it to the water when it boils. Cover and cook the rice till it is done and the water is absorbed. Serve hot with mutton or fish curry.

4. Mutton Biriyani

Mutton	*1 kg.*	*a little saffron or a pinch of yellow food colouring*	
Pulao Rice	*1 kg.*	*Garam masala powder*	*2tsp.*
Onions	*500 gm.*	*Salt*	*to taste*
Garlic	*50 gm.*	**For garam masala powder**	
Ginger	*50 gm.*	*Cinnamon*	*2 gm.*
Green chillies	*100 gm.*	*Cardamom*	*1 gm.*
Poppy seeds	*2 tsp.*	*Cloves*	*1 gm.*
Coriander leaves	*1 bunch*	*Nutmeg*	*1/4*
Mint leaves	*small bunch*	*Aniseed*	*1/2 tsp.*
Curd	*1 cup*	*Cumminseed*	*1/2 tsp.*
Juice of lime	*1*	*Cakeseed*	*1/2 tsp.*
Ghee or oil	*250 gm.*	*Mace*	*2 gm.*
Sliced cashewnuts	*20 gm.*	*All these 8 items should be dried and powdered*	
Raisins	*20 gm.*		
Rose water	*2 tbsp.*		

Cut the mutton into big pieces and wash. Slice the onion fine. Grind the chillies, garlic and poppy seeds separately. Chop the coriander leaves and mint leaves.

Heat a heavy bottomed vessel and add half of the ghee. Add half the sliced onion and fry till transparent. Add the garlic, ginger, chillies and poppyseeds, fry for 2-3 minutes. Add the mutton and fry for a few minutes more. Add the curd, salt and 1/2 cup water. Cover and cook on a slow fire.

When the mutton is half cooked, add lime juice, coriander leaves and mint leaves. Cook till the mutton is tender and the water is absorbed. Remove from the fire and keep aside.

Pick and wash the rice and drain it in a colander. Heat the remaining ghee in a vessel. Add the other half of the onion, frying it to a golden brown. Fry the cashewnuts and raisins along with the onion and remove. Add the rice and fry for 4-5 minutes. Add double the quantity of hot water, add salt and cook till the rice is soft and the water is absorbed. Remove from the fire.

Take the vessel containing mutton and sprinkle a little garam masala on top. Put one layer of cooked rice on top of the mutton. Sprinkle a little garam masala powder, fried onions, cashewnuts, raisins, and a little colouring mixed in rose water. Finish with 2 more layers of rice, garam masala, onions, cashewnuts and raisins. Cover with a heavy lid. Place some live coals on top for 15 minutes or put the dish in a hot oven for about 15 minutes.

5. Chicken Biriyani

Chicken *about 1kg.*
(cut into big pieces)
Pulao rice *1 kg.*
Onions *500 gm.*
Ghee or oil *250 gm.*
Green chillies *100 gm.*
Ginger *50 gm.*
Garlic *50 gm.*
Poppy seeds *1 tsp.*
a little saffron or a pinch of yellow food-colouring
Garam masala powder *2 tsp.*
Salt *to taste*

For garam masala powder

Cinnamon *2 gm.*
Cardamom *1 gm.*
Cloves *1 gm.*

Curd	*1 cup*	*Nutmeg*	*1/4*
Coriander leaves	*1 bunch*	*Aniseed*	*1/2 tsp.*
Mint leaves	*small bunch*	*Cumminseed*	*1/2 tsp.*
Sliced cashewnuts	*20 gm.*	*Cakeseed*	*1/2 tsp.*
Raisins	*20 gm.*	*Mace*	*2 gm.*
Juice of lime	*1*	*All these 8 items should be dried and powdered*	
Rose water	*2 tsp.*		

Slice the onion fine. Grind the green chillies, ginger, garlic and poppy seeds separately. Chop the coriander leaves and mint leaves. Heat a heavy-bottomed vessel and add half of the ghee. Add half of sliced onion and fry till transparent. Add the ginger, garlic, chillies and poppy seeds, fry for 2-3 minutes. Add the chicken and fry for a few minutes more. Add the curd, salt and 1/4 cup water. Cover and cook on a slow fire. When the chicken is half cooked, add lime juice, coriander leaves and mint leaves. Cook till the chicken is tender and the water is absorbed. Remove from the fire and keep aside.

Pick and wash the rice and drain it in a colander. Heat the remaining ghee in a vessel. Add the other half of the onion, and fry to a golden brown. Fry the cashewnuts and raisins along with the onions and remove. Add the rice and fry for about 4-5 minutes. Add double the quantity of hot water. Add salt and cook till the rice is soft and the water is absorbed. Remove from the fire.

Take the vessel containing the chicken and sprinkle a little garam masala powder on the chicken. Put one layer of cooked rice on top of the chicken masala. Sprinkle a little garam masala powder, fried onion, cashewnuts, raisins and a little colouring mixed in rose water. Finish with 2 more layers of rice in the same way. Cover with a heavy lid. Place some live coals on top for 15 minutes or put the dish in a hot oven for about 15 minutes.

6. Fish Biriyani

Seer fish	*500 gm.*	*Curd*	*1 cup*
Pulao rice	*500 gm.*	*Coriander leaves*	*1 bunch*
Onions (big)	*3*	*Mint leaves*	*½ bunch*
Green chillies	*10*	*Garam masala powder*	*3 tsp.*
Garlic	*1 pod*	*Juice of lime*	*1*
Ginger	*4 cm. piece*	*Rose water*	*1 tbsp.*
Poppy seeds	*1½ tsp.*	*Saffron*	*a pinch*
Coriander powder	*2 tsp.*	*Ghee (for pulao)*	*4 tbsp.*
Chilli powder	*2 tsp.*	*Oil*	*to fry fish*
Turmeric powder	*1 tsp.*	*Salt*	*to taste*

Pick, wash and drain the rice. Clean and wash the fish and cut it into 2 cm.-thick slices. Rub in salt, turmeric and half the chilli powder and allow the fish to marinate for a while. Heat oil and shallow fry the fish till well browned.

Slice the onions, chop coriander and mint leaves. Grind the garlic, ginger and green chillies. Grind the poppy seeds to a smooth paste. Beat the curd, add the ground poppy seeds and mix well. Soak saffron in a little rose water and keep aside.

Heat a little ghee. Add half the sliced onions and saute. Add the ground ingredients and fry for a while. Add the coriander powder, chilli powder and salt to taste. Mix well. Add the curd mixture with a little water and simmer for a while. Add the fried fish, chopped coriander leaves, mint leaves, lime juice and half the garam masala powder. Simmer on a slow fire, stirring occasionally till the gravy thickens. Remove from the fire and keep aside.

Heat the remaining ghee, add the remaining onions and fry them to a golden brown. Remove and keep aside.

Add rice and fry for about 5 minutes. Add sufficient boiling water to cook the rice. Add salt to taste. Cook till the rice is cooked and the water is completely absorbed. Transfer half the rice on to a pan, sprinkle a little garam masala powder and saffron mixture and some fried onion on top of the rice. Spread the fish masala evenly on it. Spread the other half of the rice over it and again sprinkle garam masala powder, saffron mixture and the fried onion. Cover the pan with a tight-fitting lid and put some live coals on top or place it in an oven for 10-15 minutes.

Garnish with fried onions and serve hot.

7. Prawn Biriyani

Shelled prawns	*500 gm.*	*Chilli powder*	*1 tsp.*
Pulao rice	*500 gm.*	*Turmeric powder*	*½ tsp.*
Ghee	*150 ml.*	*Garam masala powder*	*1 tsp.*
Onions	*250 gm.*	*Coriander leaves*	*1 bunch*
Green chillies	*50 gm.*	*Oil*	*200 ml.*
Garlic	*30 gm.*	*Juice of lime*	*1*
Ginger	*30 gm.*	*Salt*	*to taste*
Coriander powder	*2 tsp.*		

Clean and wash the prawns. Smear on mixture of chilli powder, turmeric powder and salt. Grind the green chillies, ginger and garlic. Slice the onion fine.

Heat the oil and fry the prawns to a light brown colour and remove. Fry half the onion in the same oil till light brown. Add the ginger, garlic and green chilli paste and fry for a few seconds. Add the coriander powder, stir well and add ½ cup water and salt to taste. When the gravy is thick, add the fried prawns, lime juice, chopped coriander leaves and garam masala powder. Stir well, remove from the fire and keep aside.

Pick, wash and drain the rice. Heat the ghee and saute the remaining onion. Add the rice and fry for a few minutes. Add sufficient hot water and salt. Cook till the rice is done and the water is absorbed.

Remove half the rice to a pan and spread prawn masala over the rice in the vessel. Spread the rest of the rice over the masala.

Cover with a lid and keep on a slow fire for a few minutes. Serve hot with coconut chutney and pappad.

8. Erachi Choru

(Mutton Pulao)

Mutton	*500 gm.*	*Green chillies*	*6*
Pulao rice	*500 gm.*	*Ginger*	*25 gm.*
Ghee	*50 ml.*	*Garlic*	*1 pod*
Onions (big)	*4*	*Cinnamon*	*7 cm. piece*
Cloves	*6*	*Coriander leaves*	*1 bunch*
Cardamom	*6 pods*	*Juice of lime*	*1*
Coriander powder	*1 tbsp.*	*Oil*	*50 ml.*
Turmeric powder	*½ tsp.*	*Salt*	*to taste*
Chilli powder	*1 tsp.*		

Cut the mutton into medium-size pieces and wash. Slice the onion finely. Crush the chillies, ginger and garlic. Chop the coriander leaves. Heat the oil, add half the cinnamon, cardamom, cloves and onion. Fry till the onion is transparent. Add the ginger, garlic and green chilli paste. Fry till an aroma rises. Add the mutton and all the other ingredients. Fry for a few minutes. Add 1 cup water, salt and lime juice. Cover and cook till the mutton is soft and the water is absorbed. Keep aside.

Wash and drain the rice. Heat the ghee. Add the remaining cinnamon, cardamom, cloves and onion. Fry till the onion is transparent. Add rice and fry for few minutes. Add salt and sufficient hot water to cook the rice.

Cook till the rice is done and the water is absorbed. Remove half the rice from the vessel and add the mutton. Add the rest of the rice. Mix the rice and mutton together well. Serve hot with chutney and pickle.

9. Chakkara Choru

(Sweet Wheatgrain Pulao)

Wheat (cleaned and prepared preferably Chamba wheat) 200 gm.	*Jaggery*	*100 gm.*
	Coconut	*1*
	Salt	*a little*

Pick and clean the wheat. Sprinkle a little water on the wheat and mix it well with your hands. Pound and de-husk the wheat. Winnow and remove the husk and small grains.

Grate the coconut and take out the first and second milk separately.

Cook the wheat in the second milk till it is very soft. Add jaggery and a little salt. Cook till the jaggery is well mixed. Add the first milk and stir. Simmer for a few minutes till it reaches a thick consistency. Remove from the fire.

10. Gothamba Choru

(Sweet Wheatgrain Rice)

Wheat (cleaned and prepared Chamba wheat)	*500 gm.*	*Chopped small onion (sambar onion)*	*2 tsp.*
Grated coconut	*1 cup*	*Ghee*	*4 tsp.*
		Sugar	*4 tbsp.*

Prepare the wheat as in the previous recipe. Cook the wheat in sufficient water till it is soft and the water is absorbed.

Add the grated coconut, sugar and a little salt. Stir and keep on a slow fire till the sugar melts and blends with the wheat. Remove from the fire and keep aside. Heat the ghee and fry the onions till golden brown. Remove from the fire. Add the onions with ghee to the wheat and stir well. Serve hot.

PATHIRIS, PUTTUS AND SOUPS

11. Podi Pathiri

(Rice Flour Chapati)

Rice flour	*500 gm.*	*Thick coconut milk*	
Water	*½ litre*	*Salt*	*to taste*

Boil the water with salt. When the water boils put in the flour, make a hole in the centre by placing a long handled spoon in the liquid. Cover with a lid and keep on a slow fire for a minute. Uncover and stir till well mixed. Remove from the fire.

Cool and knead the mixture to a soft dough without adding any water. Make small balls. Sprinkle rice flour and roll out the balls into very thin chapatis. Cut with a round cutter (to make the discs even). Heat a tava and place a chapati on it. After a few seconds turn it over. Repeat this once more. When it puffs up remove it from the tava. Dip each chapati in coconut milk on one side just before serving.

Serve with mutton or chicken stew.

N. B. The term boiled rice in the folowing recipes refers to the parboiled rice sold in the market, not cooked rice.

12. Arippathiri

(Ground Rice Chapati)

Boiled rice	*500 gm.*	*Water*	*½ litre*
Thick coconut milk	*½ cup*	*Ghee*	*2 tbsp.*
Salt	*to taste*		

Pick and clean the rice. Boil the water. When the water boils, add the rice and remove from the fire. Cover with a tight-fitting lid; keep aside. After half an hour open and stir the mixture. Set aside for 3-4 hours. Drain off the water, wash with cold water and drain. Add salt to taste and grind it to a smooth thick paste, adding very little water.

Oil your hand well. Take some rice paste and shape it into a ball as big as an orange and flatten it to a chapati shape of ¼ inch thickness onto a cloth or banana leaf. Heat a tava, put the chapati on it and remove the cloth or leaf. After two minutes turn it over and let it cook for two minutes again. Repeat this 2-3 times more, then slightly press it with a piece of crumpled paper so that it puffs up. Turn it over and press the other side in the same way. Remove from the tava. Make similar pathiris (8-9) with the rest of the dough. Melt the ghee and add the coconut milk. Dip each pathiri in the coconut milk and serve hot with mutton or fish curry.

Meen Pathiri

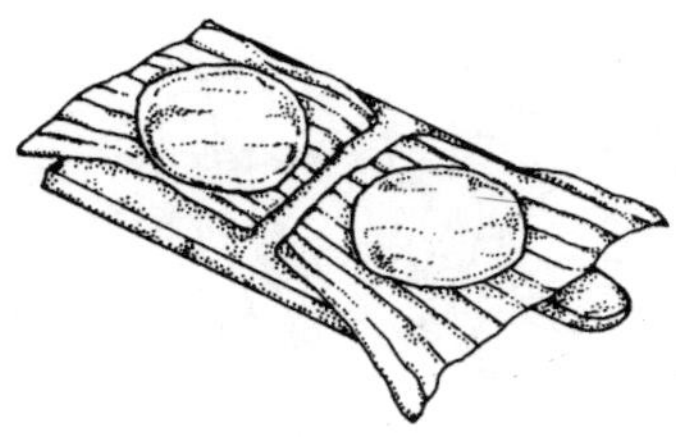

1. With greased hands, place the two balls of dough on two banana leaf pieces and flatten into two chapatis of quarter-inch thickness (pathiris).

2. Fill one pathiri with the fish masala and gently place the other pathiri on top.

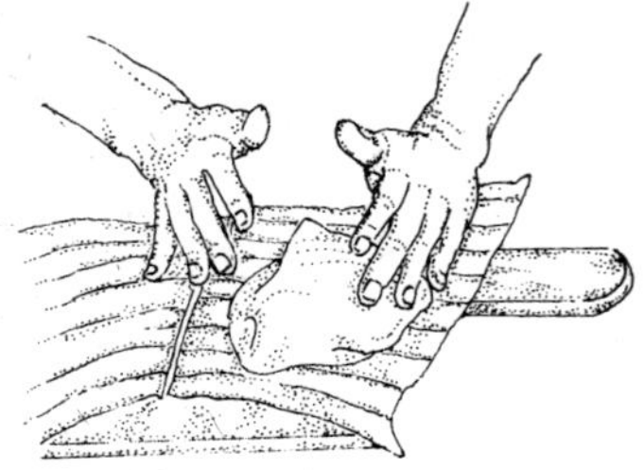

3. Seal the edges of the pathiris with greased fingers. Place the pathiris with the banana leaves in an idli vessel on the fire. Steam for about half an hour or until cooked.

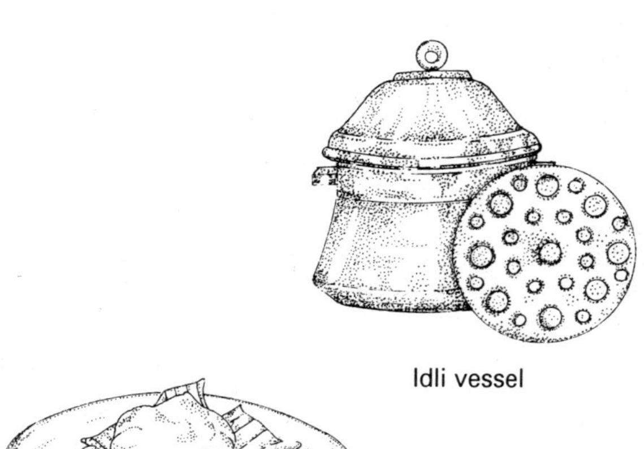

Idli vessel

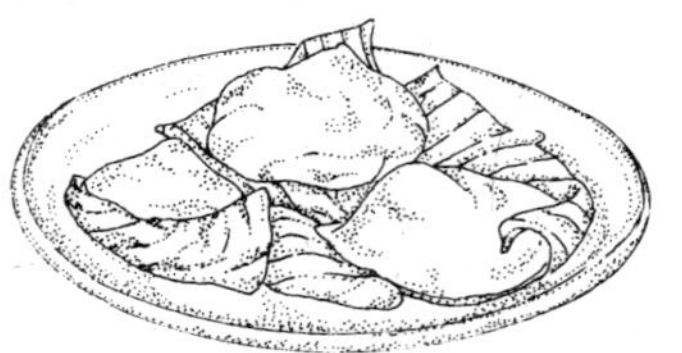

13. Meen Pathiri

(Steamed Rice-pie with fish)

For the Pathiri

Boiled rice	*500 gm.*	*Small onion (peeled)*	*50 gm.*
Coconut, grated	*½*	*Cardamom*	*2 pods*
Aniseed	*1 tsp.*	*Big sections of banana leaf*	*2*
Cumminseed	*1 tsp.*	*Salt*	*to taste*

For the stuffing

Pomfret or seer fish	*½ kg.*	*Cinnamon*	*4 cm. piece*
Onions (big)	*2*	*Cloves*	*3*
Green chillies	*4*	*Cardamom*	*2 pods*
Ginger	*1 cm. piece*	*Aniseed*	*½ tsp.*
Garlic	*½ pod*	*Coriander leaves*	*½ bunch*
Coriander powder	*1 tbsp.*	*Curry leaves*	*1 sprig*
Chilli powder	*1 tsp.*	*Oil*	*2 tbsp.*
Turmeric powder	*½ tsp.*	*Salt*	*to taste*
Grated coconut	*2 tbsp.*		

Clean and soak the rice in hot water for 4-5 hours. Wash and drain it. Add the coconut, aniseed, cumminseed, cardamom, small onion and salt to the rice and grind it to a thick smooth paste, adding very little water. Keep aside.

To make the stuffing: Cut the fish into big slices and wash thoroughly. Apply a little chilli powder, turmeric powder and salt. Shallow fry in hot oil and keep aside. Slice the onions and chillies. Grind the ginger and garlic. Chop coriander leaves. Grind 2 tbsp. coconut to a smooth paste with aniseed, cinnamon, cardamom and cloves.

Heat 2 tbsp. oil and saute onion and chillies. When the

onion becomes transparent add ginger and garlic. Stir for a while and add coriander, chilli and turmeric powder. Stir well and add ½ cup water. Mix the ground coconut in ½cup water, add to the masala and simmer for a while. When the gravy thickens add the fried fish and keep on the fire for few minutes more, shaking the pan occasionally. Add the coriander and curry leaves, remove from the fire and cool.

To make the Pathiri: Oil your hands and shape the rice dough into balls the size of a small orange and flatten it on a piece of banana leaf to a chapati ¼ inch thick. Make one more pathiri in the same way. Place a piece of fish and some masala on one pathiri and spread it evenly. Cover with another pathiri. Press the edges well with oiled fingers. Make 4 or 5 pathiris in the same way with the remaining rice paste and fish masala.

Place an idli vessel on the fire. Put the inner lid in it (this is a lid with holes). Arrange three or four pathiris in it on banana leaves. Steam till cooked. Remove and cool. Peel off the leaves and serve.

14. Neippathiri

(Rice Poori)

Boiled rice	*500 gm.*	*Coconut, grated*	½
Aniseed	*1 tsp.*	*Oil*	*for deep frying*
Salt	*to taste*		

Pick. clean and soak the rice in hot water for 4-5 hours. Wash and drain the rice. Add the coconut, aniseed and salt. Grind the rice to a smooth thick, paste, adding very little water.

Oil your hand and make small balls of rice paste.

Flaten each ball like a poori on a piece of cloth or a banana leaf. Heat oil. Remove the poori from the leaf and put it in the hot oil. Fry to a golden brown. Remove and drain. Serve hot with mutton curry.

15. Puzungalorotti

(Steamed Rice-cake Cuts)

Boiled rice	*500 gm.*	*Cumminseed*	*1 tsp.*
Coconut, grated	*3/4*	*Cardamom*	*4 pods*
Onions (small)	*50 gm.*	*Ghee*	*2 tbsp.*
Aniseed	*1 tsp.*	*Salt*	*to taste*

Pick, clean and soak the rice in hot water for 2-3 hours. Peel and chop the onions. Add the rice, coconut, cumminseeds, aniseed, chopped onions, cardamom and salt. Grind to a smooth paste.

Add enough water to make a batter of pouring consistency. Grease a vessel with 2 tablespoons ghee. Pour the batter into it and steam it till cooked. Remove and cool. Cut into the desired shapes. Serve with chicken or mutton masala.

16. Adukkoroti

(Layered Rice Chapati)

Raw rice (preferably pulao rice)	*200 gm.*	*Boiled rice*	*200 gm.*
		Ghee	*100 gm.*
Coconut, grated	*1/2*	*Cardamom*	*3 pods*
Egg	*1*	*Salt*	*to taste*

Pick, clean and soak both rices together in cold water for 2-3 hours. Wash and drain the rice in a colander and add the grated coconut. Grind the rice mixture to a very smooth paste adding a little water. Add the egg and beat the rice mixture with a wooden masher or egg beater till it is frothy. Add more water to make a thin batter as for pancakes. Beat well again. Add powdered cardamom and salt.

Take a small vessel and grease it well with 2 tsp. ghee. Pour 2 or 3 tablespoons of the batter into the greased vessel. Steam till it is done. Spread 2 teaspoon ghee evenly over the cooked layer. Beat the batter well again and pour 3 tablespoons rice batter on top of the cooked layer. Cover and cook till done. Continue the same procedure till all the rice batter is used up. Cook till it is done. Remove the vessel and cool it. Keep it slightly tilted to remove the excess ghee. Turn onto a plate.

Cut and serve with chicken or mutton masala.

17. Arikkadukka

(Stuffed Mussels)

Water mussels (medium-sized)	*25*
Boiled rice	*400 gm.*
Coconut, grated	*½*
Aniseed	*2 tsp.*
Cumminseed	*1 tsp.*
Peeled onion (small)	*½ cup*
Oil	*for frying*
Salt	*to taste*

For masala

Chilli powder	*2 tbsp.*
Turmeric powder	*½ tsp.*
Garlic	*5 cloves*
Aniseed	*1 tsp.*
Salt	*to taste*

Scrape and remove all the dirt from the mussels. Wash them several times in cold water till completely clean. Drain in a basket. Cut each one halfway down. Keep aside in the basket to remove excess water.

Soak rice in hot water. Close with a lid and keep aside for 4-5 hours. Wash and drain the rice. Add all the ingredients, except oil, to the rice and grind the rice to a smooth thick paste.

Stuff each mussel neatly with rice paste. Steam it till done. Remove from the fire and cool it till you can handle it. Remove the shell. Mix the ground masala in a little water and make a thin batter. Heat oil. Dip each mussel in masala and shallow fry a few at a time in hot oil till done. Remove and drain.

18. Poori

Wheat flour	*400 gm.*	*Oil*	*for frying*
Ghee	*2 tbsp.*	*Salt*	*to taste*

Melt ghee and add the flour. Add salt and water and prepare a stiff dough. Knead well. Divide into even-sized balls. Roll out very thin (about 1 mm. thickness) 8 cm. round in diameter.

Fry in hot oil, gently pressing down with a flat spoon. When puffed up turn over. Lightly brown on both sides. Remove and drain. Serve hot.

19. Paratha

Wholemeal		*Ghee*	*115 gm.*

flour	*450 gm.*
Salt	*to taste*

Rub part of the ghee into the flour. Add salt and water and make a dough. Keep aside for half an hour. Knead well. Divide into even-sized portions. Roll out each 5 mm. thick. Smear ghee over these. Fold into two and again fold into two to make it square. Roll out into square shapes.

Heat tava and bake each paratha for a minute. Add ghee around the edges and little on top. Turn over and cook both the sides.

20. Puttu

(Steamed Rice Cakes)

Raw rice	*500 gm.*	*Coconut, grated*	*1/2*
Salt	*to taste*		

Clean and soak the rice in cold water for 2-3 hours. Drain till the moisture is absorbed. Pound and sieve with a medium sieve. Roast the flour and cool. Add salted water little by little and mix with fingers till it forms small grains. Keep this aside for half an hour. Boil water in a *puttu vessel* (specially made for this). Take a *puttu kutti* (a long cylindrical vessel) sprinkle a little coconut and then put a handful of the prepared flour. Proceed thus till the *kutti* is filled, finishing with a layer of coconut on top. Keep it in the *puttu* vessel and cover with the lid. Cook till the steam comes out. Remove *kutti* from the vessel, place it on a plate and push out the contents with a

Idi Puttu

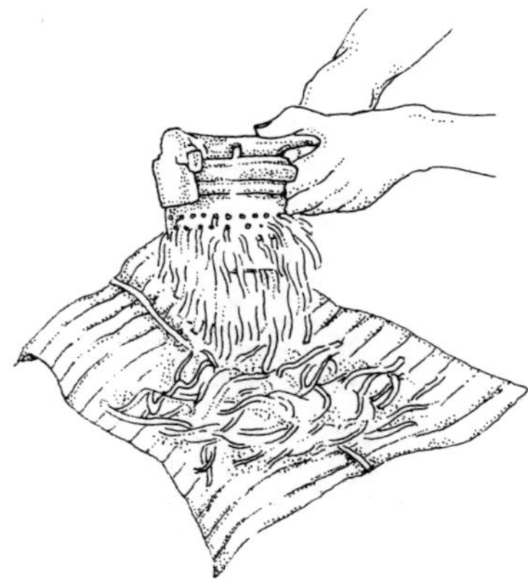

1. Fill mould (with medium holes) with stiff dough. Keeping a plantain leaf or plate below, press the mould handle to make idiappam. Sprinkle rice flour on the idiappam.

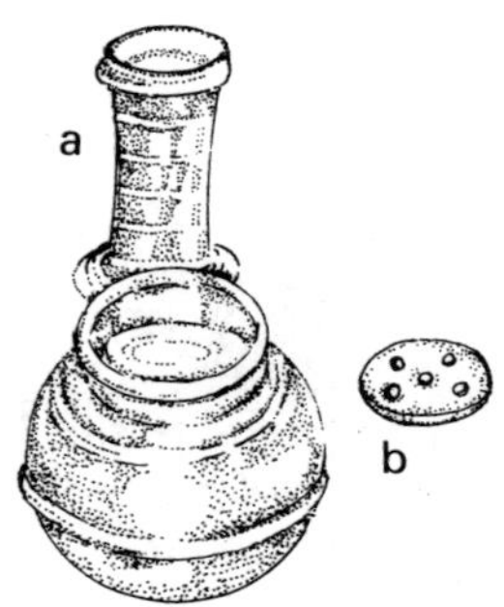

2. a. kutti – the vertical spout
   b. perforated plate

3. Arrange alternate layers of idiappam and grated coconut in the kutti and cook till steam comes out of the kutti.

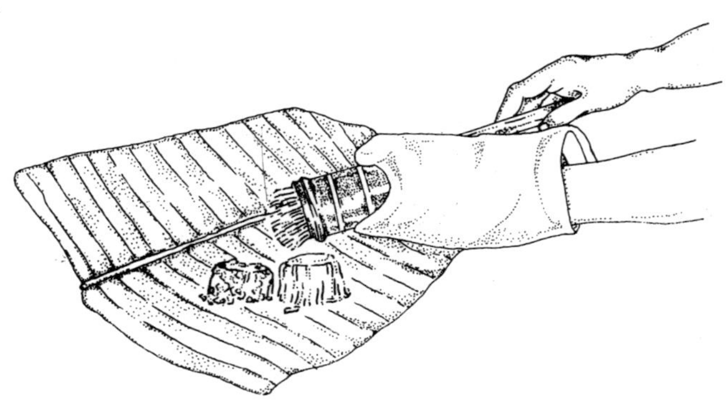

4. Remove the kutti from the vessel and push out the steamed puttu with a rolling pin onto a plate.

chapati rolling pin. Serve hot with Fish Curry or Fish Varattiyathu.

21. Idi Puttu

(Steamed Rice-noodle Cakes)

Raw rice	*500 gm.*	*Water*	*½ litre*
Coconut	*1*	*Salt*	*to taste*

Prepare the flour the same way as for the previous recipe but sieve it with a fine sieve. Boil ½ litre water. When water boils add flour, reduce heat and stir till well mixed. Remove from fire. If the dough is very stiff add a little more hot water. Knead to a stiff dough. Take a little dough, put in an *idiappam* mould with medium holes and press it on a thali sprinkled with rice flour. Sprinkle a little rice flour on the pressed *idi.* Press another layer of *idi.* Finish all the dough the same way. Toss lightly with your fingers to prevent it from sticking. Grate and crush half a coconut and extract 1 cup thick milk. Add sugar and a pinch of salt. If desired add two bananas cut into small pieces.

The method of making puttu is same as in the previous recipe. Serve hot with coconut milk and sugar or Kari.

22. Meen Puttu

(Steamed Rice and Fish Cakes)

Rice flour	*500 gm.*	*Onion (big)*	*1*
Salmon	*6*	*Green chillies*	*4*

or		*Curry leaves*	*1 sprig*
Seer fish	*250 gm.*	*Salt*	*to taste*
Ginger	*2 cm. piece*		
Coriander leaves	*1 bunch*		

Prepare the rice flour as for Puttu. Clean and wash the fish. Cook the fish in a little water with salt to taste. Remove and flake the flesh. Chop the onion, chillies, ginger and coriander leaves. Heat the ghee and saute the onion and chillies. Add the ginger and flaked fish. Add coriander leaves and curry leaves and remove from the fire.

Put 2 tbsp. fish masala in the *kutti,* then one handful rice flour. Fill the *kutti* the same way finishing with a layer of fish. Cover and cook till the steam comes out.

23. Erachi Puttu

(Steamed Rice and Meat Cakes)

Rice flour	*500 gm.*	*Coriander powder*	*2 tsp.*
Minced mutton	*250 gm.*	*Chilli powder*	*½ tsp.*
Onions (big)	*2*	*Turmeric powder*	*¼ tsp.*
Green chillies	*4*	*Garam masala powder*	*¼ tsp.*
Ginger paste	*½ tsp.*	*Coriander leaves*	*½ bunch*
Garlic paste	*1 tsp.*	*Oil*	*2 tbsp.*

Prepare the rice flour as for Puttu. Cook mince with coriander powder, chilli powder, turmeric powder and salt till the meat is soft and the water is absorbed. Chop onion, green chillies and coriander leaves. Heat oil and saute onion and chillies. Add ginger and garlic paste and fry for a while. Add mince, coriander leaves and garam masala powder. Fry for few seconds more and remove from the fire.

Follow the same procedure as for Meen puttu and Idi puttu.

24. Kanji

(Rice Soup with Coconut Milk)

Broken rice	*250 gm.*	*Salt*	*to taste*
Grated coconut	*150 gm.*		

Wash and cook rice in sufficient water. Cook till the rice is very soft. Crush coconut and take out 1 cup thick milk. Add to the rice soup and salt to taste. Serve with coconut chutney.

25. Jeeraka Kanji 1

(Cummin Flavour Rice Soup)

Rice (preferably pulao rice)	*250 gm.*	*Turmeric powder*	*¼ tsp.*
Coconut	*½*	*Chopped onion (small)*	*1 tbsp.*
Cumminseed	*2 tsp.*	*salt*	*to taste*

Grind coconut to a smooth paste with jeera, turmeric and onion. Wash and cook the rice in sufficient water till well cooked. Mash the rice thoroughly. Add the ground coconut and sufficient water. 2 tsp. ghee may be added if preferred.

Boil again for a few minutes and remove from the fire.

26. Jeeraka Kanji 2

(Cummin Flavour Rice Soup)

Rice (preferably pulao rice)	*250 gm.*	*Turmeric powder*	*¼ tsp.*
Coconut	*½*	*Chopped onion (small)*	*2 tbsp.*
Cumminseed	*2 tsp.*	*Salt*	*to taste*

Grind coconut to a smooth paste with jeera, turmeric and onion. Wash and cook the rice in sufficient water till the rice is very soft. Add the ground coconut mixed in 1 cup water. Boil for few minutes and remove from the fire. Add salt to taste.

27. Gothamba Kanji 1

(Mashed Wheat Soup)

Prepared wheat (pounded and husked)	*200 gm.*	*Onion (big)*	*1*
Mutton or chicken	*100 gm.*	*Chopped onion (small)*	*1 tbsp.*
Small coconut	*1*	*Ghee*	*1 tbsp.*
or big coconut	*½*	*Salt*	*to taste*

Wash and cook the wheat along with the mutton and sliced onion. Cook till the wheat is very soft.

Crush coconut and extract 2 cups thick first milk and

2 cups second milk. Keep aside.

When the wheat is well cooked remove from the fire. Remove all the mutton pieces and shred finely. Mash the wheat well and pass it through a pulper, adding the second milk little by little. Add first milk, mutton and salt to taste. Heat ghee and fry chopped onions to a golden brown. Add to the prepared kanji and heat it.

Serve hot with pickles or chutney.

28. Gothamba Kanji 2

(Wheatgrain Soup)

Prepared wheat	*200 gm.*	*Onion (big)*	*1*
Small coconut	*1*	*Salt*	*to taste*
or big coconut	*1/2*		

Wash and cook the wheat with sliced onion. Cook till the wheat is very soft. Extract coconut milk and add to the cooked soup. Stir well and boil. Add salt to taste and remove from the fire.

29. Alisa

(Wheat Potage with Meat)

Chamba wheat (prepared)	*200 gm.*	*Onion (big)*	*1*
Chicken or mutton	*1/4 kg.*	*Cinnamon*	*4 cm. piece*
Chopped small onion (sambar onion)	*2 tsp.*	*Ghee*	*4 tbsp.*

Cook the wheat with chicken, big onion and cinnamon in

sufficient water till the wheat is very soft. Remove from the fire and mash it well with a wooden *mandh* (dal-masher buttermilk churner) till it is well mashed and looks like porridge. Keep it aside. Heat ghee and fry chopped onion till golden brown. Remove from fire. Add the ghee and onion to the mashed wheat and stir. Serve hot with more ghee and sugar.

30. Kiskiya

(Whole Wheat Porridge)

Chamba wheat (prepared)	*200 gm.*	*Cinnamon*	*4 cm. piece*
Minced mutton	*100 gm.*	*Ghee*	*2 tbsp.*
Coconut	*1/2*	*Salt*	*to taste*
Chopped onion (small)	*2 tsp.*		

Wash the wheat. Cook it in sufficient water with mutton and cinnamon. Grate coconut and take out the first and second milk separately. Keep this aside. When the wheat is half cooked add the second milk and cook till the wheat is very soft. Add the first milk and salt. Simmer for a few minutes. Remove from the fire. Heat the ghee and fry the onion to a golden brown. Remove from the fire and add to the cooked wheat. Serve hot with sugar.

31. Kichri

Green gram dal (moong dal)	*200 gm.*	*Coconut*	*1/2*
		Chopped onion	*1tbsp.*

Raw rice	*150 gm.*	*(small)*	
(preferably pulao rice)		*Ghee*	*2 tbsp.*
		Salt	*to taste*

Pick, clean and wash rice and dal. Cook rice and dal together in sufficient water till rice is done and water is absorbed. Grate coconut and extract 1 cup thick milk. When dal and rice are almost cooked add coconut milk and salt. Cook till done. Remove from the fire. Heat the ghee and fry the chopped onion golden brown. Remove from the fire. Add ghee along with the onions to the cooked dal and rice. Serve hot with more ghee and sugar.

MEAT

32. Mutton Curry 1

Mutton	*250 gm.*	*Tomatoes*	*2*
Onions (big)	*2*	*Potatoes*	*2*
Green chillies	*4*	*Cinnamon*	*4 cm. piece*
Aniseed	*1 tsp.*	*Cloves*	*3*
Ginger	*4 cm. piece*	*Coriander leaves*	*½ bunch*
Garlic	*1 pod*	*Ghee or oil*	*2 tbsp.*
Coriander powder	*2 tbsp.*	*Curry leaves*	*few sprigs*
Turmeric powder	*½ tsp.*	*Salt*	*to taste*
Chilli powder	*½ tsp.*		

Clean and cut the mutton into convenient sized pieces. Wash the mutton. Slice the onions, chillies and tomatoes. Chop the coriander leaves. Peel and cut the potatoes into four. Grind the ginger, garlic and aniseed.

Heat the ghee. Add the cloves, cinnamon, onions, chillies and curry leaves. Fry till the onions are transparent. Add the ground paste and fry till the aroma comes. Add coriander powder, turmeric powder, chilli powder, mutton and salt. Fry for a few minutes more till the masala is lightly browned. Add sufficient water. Add the tomatoes and potatoes. Cook till the mutton is soft and gravy thickens. Add coriander leaves and remove from the fire.

33. Mutton Curry 2

Mutton	*250 gm.*	*Chilli powder*	*1/2 tsp.*
Onions (big)	*2*	*Aniseed*	*1 tsp.*
Green chillies	*4*	*Cloves*	*3*
Ginger	*4 cm. piece*	*Cinnamon*	*4 cm. piece*
Garlic	*1/2 pod*	*Coriander leaves*	*1/2 bunch*
Tomatoes	*2*	*Oil*	*2 tbsp.*
Potatoes	*2*	*Curry leaves*	*1 sprig*
Coriander powder	*2 tbsp.*	*Salt*	*to taste*
Turmeric powder	*1/2 tsp.*		

Clean and cut the mutton into convenient-sized pieces and wash. Slice the onion, chillies and tomatoes. Peel and cut the potatoes into four. Grind the ginger, garlic and aniseed. Chop the coriander leaves. Mix the mutton with the onion, green chillies, coriander powder, chilli powder, turmeric powder, ground masala and salt, and keep it aside for 15 minutes. Heat the ghee. Add the cloves, cinnamon and curry leaves. When the spices brown add mutton and fry till the masala is lightly browned. Add sufficient water, tomatoes, potatoes and salt.

Cook till the mutton is soft and the gravy thickens. Add coriander leaves and remove from the fire.

34. Mutton Curry 3

Mutton	*250 gm.*	*Chilli powder*	*1 tsp.*
Grated coconut	*1½ cups*	*Tomatoes*	*2*
Aniseed	*1 tsp.*	*Potatoes*	*2*
Onions (big)	*2*	*Cloves*	*3*
Green chillies	*4*	*Cinnamon*	*4 cm. piece*
Ginger	*4 cm. piece*	*Coriander leaves*	*½ bunch*
Garlic	*½ pod*	*Ghee or oil*	*2 tbsp.*
Coriander powder	*1½ tbsp.*	*Curry leaves*	*few sprigs*
Turmeric powder	*1 tsp.*	*Salt*	*to taste*

Clean, cut and wash the mutton. Slice onion, chillies and tomatoes. Peel and cut the potatoes into four. Grind the ginger and garlic. Roast the coconut with aniseed and a little turmeric powder in 1 tsp. oil to a golden brown. Grind this to a fine paste and keep aside. Add the onions, chillies, ginger and garlic paste, chilli powder, turmeric powder, coriander powder and salt to the mutton and mix well. Heat the ghee. Add the spices and curry leaves. Add the mutton and fry till the masala is lightly browned. Add enough water to cook the mutton. Add the potatoes and tomatoes. Cook till the mutton is soft. Mix the ground coconut with a little water. Add to the curry. Add chopped coriander leaves. Simmer for few minutes and remove from fire.

35. Mutton Stew 1

Mutton	*250 gm.*	*Green chillies*	*6*
Coconut	*1/2*	*Garlic pod*	*1/2*
Onions (big)	*2*	*Ginger*	*2 cm. piece*
Potatoes	*2*	*Coriander leaves*	*1/2 bunch*
Tomatoes	*2*	*Juice of lime*	*1/2*
Cinnamon	*4 cm. piece*	*Ghee or oil*	*2 tbsp.*
Cardamom	*2 pods*	*Salt*	*to taste*
Cloves	*3*		

Wash and cut the mutton into medium-sized pieces. Slice the onions, tomatoes and chillies. Grind together garlic and ginger. Peel and cut the potatoes into four. Chop the coriander leaves. Heat the oil. Add the sliced onion, chillies, cinnamon, cloves and cardamoms, and saute. Add the ginger garlic paste and fry for a while. Add the meat and fry for a few minutes more. Add just enough water to cook meat. Add the potatoes, tomatoes and salt to taste. Cook till the mutton is tender and the water is absorbed. Grate the coconut and take out 1 1/2 cups thick milk. Add the milk and coriander leaves to the meat. Simmer and remove from the fire, sprinkle lime juice and serve.

36. Mutton Stew 2

Mutton	*250 gm.*	*Potatoes*	*2*
Coconut	*1/2*	*Cloves*	*3*

Onions (big)	*2*	*Tomatoes*	*2*
Green chillies	*6*	*Coriander seeds*	*1 tbsp.*
Garlic pod	*1/2*	*Coriander leaves*	*1/2 bunch*
Ginger	*4 cm. piece*	*Ghee or oil*	*2 tbsp.*
Poppy seeds	*1 tsp.*	*Juice of lime*	*1/2*
Cinnamon	*4 cm. piece*	*Salt*	*to taste*

Clean, cut and wash the mutton. Slice the onion, chillies and tomatoes. Peel and cut the potatoes into four. Grind the coriander seeds and poppy seeds separately to a fine paste. Grind the ginger and garlic together. Add the onions, chillies, ground masala and salt to the mutton and mix well.

Heat the ghee and add spices. Add the mutton and fry for a while. Add just sufficient water to cook the mutton. Cook the mutton till soft and water is absorbed. Grate the coconut and take out 2 cups of milk. Add the milk and chopped coriander leaves. Simmer and remove from the fire. Add lime juice and serve hot.

37. Erachi Porichathu

(Fried Mutton)

Mutton	*250 gm.*	*Garlic*	*1 pod*
Chilli powder	*2 tbsp.*	*Salt*	*to taste*
Turmeric powder	*1/2 tsp.*	*Oil*	*for frying*
Aniseed	*2 tsp.*		

Clean, cut and wash the mutton. Grind the aniseed and garlic. Cook the mutton with all ingredients in just sufficient water till the mutton is tender and water is absorbed. Heat the oil. Add the mutton and fry on a low heat till the mutton is brown and oil comes out.

38. Erachi Varattiyathu

(Mutton Masala Curry)

Mutton	*250 gm.*	*Tomatoes*	*2*
Coriander powder	*2 tsp.*	*Garam masala powder*	*1 tsp.*
Chilli powder	*1 tsp.*	*Coriander leaves*	*½ bunch*
Turmeric powder	*½ tsp.*	*Oil or ghee*	*4 tbsp.*
Onions (big)	*3*	*Sugar*	*2 tsp.*
Green chillies	*4*	*Lime*	*½*
Ginger	*4 cm. piece*		
Garlic	*1 pod*		
Aniseed	*1 tsp.*		

Clean and cut the mutton into big pieces. Wash. Slice the onion fine. Grind the green chillies, ginger, garlic, coriander powder and aniseed separately. Chop the coriander leaves and tomatoes. Heat the oil. Add the onion and fry till lightly browned. Add the ground ingredients, chilli powder and turmeric powder and fry till the aroma comes. Add the mutton and fry for few minutes more (till the oil comes out). Add just enough water to cook the mutton. Add the tomatoes and salt. Cook till the mutton is soft. Add the coriander leaves, sugar, lime juice and garam masala powder. Simmer till the gravy is thick Remove from the fire and serve hot.

39. Erachi Chuttathu

(Baked Mutton)

Mutton	*500 gm.*	*Turmeric powder*	*½ tsp.*
Onions	*250 gm.*	*Raisins*	*2 tbsp.*
Green chillies	*8*	*Cashewnuts*	*2 tbsp.*
Ginger	*8 cm. piece*	*Aniseed*	*1 tbsp.*
Garlic	*2 pods*	*Garam masala powder*	*2 tsp.*
Coriander powder	*2 tbsp.*	*Coriander leaves*	*1 bunch*
Chilli powder	*1 tsp.*	*Lime*	*1*
		Ghee or oil	*100 ml.*
		Salt	*to taste*

Clean and cut the mutton into big pieces and wash. Slice the onion finely. Grind the ginger, garlic, aniseed, green chillies and coriander powder.

Heat the ghee. Add half of the onion and fry to a golden brown and remove. Fry the cashewnuts and raisins. Remove and keep aside. Add the remaining onion and fry till transparent. Add the ground ingredients, chilli powder and turmeric powder. Fry till an aroma rises. Add the mutton and fry for a few minutes more till oil comes out. Add 1 cup water and salt. Cover the vessel with a tight-fitting lid and cook on a low fire. Crush half of the fried onions and keep the other half for garnishing.

When the mutton is half cooked add the crushed onion. Cover and put some live coals on top of the lid.

Cook till all the mutton is tender and the moisture is completely absorbed.

Remove from the fire. Sprinkle lime juice and garam masala powder. Garnish with fried onions, cashewnuts and raisins.

40. Kheema Curry

Minced meat	*250 gm.*	*Chilli powder*	*1 tsp.*
Onions (big)	*2*	*Turmeric powder*	*½ tsp.*
Green chillies	*4*	*Garam masala powder*	*1tsp.*
Garlic paste	*1 tsp.*	*Tomatoes*	*2*
Ginger paste	*1 tsp.*	*Coriander leaves*	*½ bunch*
Coriander powder	*2 tsp.*	*Salt*	*to taste*

Wash and drain the minced mutton. Chop the onion, green chillies and tomatoes. Heat the oil and fry the onion and green chillies. Fry till the onions are transparent. Add the ginger and garlic paste and fry till the aroma rises. Add the mutton and all the other ingredients except coriander leaves and garam masala powder. Fry for few minutes more. Add ½ cup water and salt. Cook on a low fire till the mince is well cooked. When done add coriander leaves and garam masala powder.

41. Mutton Khorma

Mutton	*250 gm.*	*Poppy seeds*	*1 tsp.*
Onions (big)	*2*	*Curd*	*½ cup*
Green chillies	*4*	*Tomatoes (small)*	*2*
Ginger	*4 cm. piece*	*Cinnamon*	*4 cm. piece*
Garlic	*½ pod*	*Cardamom*	*2 pods*
Grated coconut	*1 cup*	*Cloves*	*4*
Coriander powder	*1 tbsp.*	*Aniseed*	*1 tsp.*
		Oil	*3 tbsp.*

Chilli powder	*1 tsp.*	*Salt*	*to taste*
Turmeric powder	*1/2 tsp.*		

Cut and wash the mutton. Slice the onion finely. Grind the ginger, garlic and green chillies separately. Grind the coconut to a smooth paste with aniseed and poppy seed. Cut the tomatoes and coriander leaves.

Heat the oil, add cinnamon, cloves and cardamom. Add the onion and green chillies. Fry for some time. Add the mutton, ginger and garlic paste, coriander powder, chilli powder and turmeric powder. Fry for a few seconds more. Add the curd, tomatoes, salt and 2 cups of water. Cook till the mutton is soft. Add the ground coconut mixed in little water. Simmer and remove from the fire. Add the coriander leaves.

42. Kaya with Mutton

(Banana with Mutton)

Malabar bananas	*2*	*Chilli powder*	*2 tsp.*
or any other variety		*Turmeric powder*	*1/2 tsp.*
Mutton	*200 gm.*	*Aniseed*	*1 tsp.*
Coconut	*1/2*	*Cloves*	*4*
Coriander powder	*2 tsp.*	*Curry leaves*	*2 sprigs*

Peel and cut the bananas, first lengthwise, then slantwise into two-inch long pieces. Wash well with a little salt. Cut mutton into small pieces and wash. Cook the bananas with mutton and turmeric, chilli and coriander powders till done. Grind the coconut to a smooth paste with aniseed and garlic. Mix it with a little water and add to the cooked banana. Add the curry leaves. Simmer and remove from the fire.

43. Stuffed Chicken

1 medium-sized chicken

For stuffing

Bengal gram dal	*½ cup*
Hard-boiled egg	*1*
Onions (big)	*2*
Garlic paste	*1 tsp.*
Ginger paste	*1 tsp.*
Coriander powder	*2 tsp.*
Turmeric powder	*¼ tsp.*
Green chillies	*4*
Garam masala powder	*½tsp.*
Raisins	*1 tsp.*
Chopped cashewnuts	*2 tbsp.*

For gravy

Onions (big)	*2*
Green chillies	*4*
Ginger paste	*1 tsp.*
Garlic paste	*1 tsp.*
Coriander powder	*2 tbsp.*
Chilli powder	*1 tsp.*
Turmeric powder	*½ tsp.*
Aniseed	*1 tsp.*
Garam masala powder	*1tsp.*
Coriander leaves	*½ bunch*
Sugar	*2 tsp.*
Oil	*3 tbsp.*

Coriander leaves	*½ bunch*	*Lime*	*½*
Sugar	*2 tsp.*	*Salt*	*to taste*
Oil	*1 tsp.*		
Salt	*to taste*		

Clean and prepare the chicken whole.

The stuffing
Wash and cook the dal with coriander powder and turmeric powder till soft and till the water is absorbed. Slice the onion and chillies. Heat the ghee and fry the onions till transparent. Add the ginger and garlic paste and green chillies and fry for a few seconds more. Add the cooked dal, chopped coriander leaves, sugar and garam masala powder. Stir well and remove from the fire. Stuff the chicken with the masala and whole hard-boiled egg. Push both the legs through the tail end and stitch the legs together. Keep the chicken aside.

The gravy
Slice onions and chillies. Grind aniseed and chop coriander leaves. Heat oil. Add onions and chillies, and saute. Add coriander powder, chilli powder and turmeric powder. Stir well and add 2 cups of water and salt to taste. Put in the chicken. Cook on a slow fire. Turn the chicken occassionally. Cook till the chicken is tender and gravy thickens. Add sugar, lime juice, garam masala powder and coriander leaves. Remove from the fire. Take off the stitches before serving.

44. Stuffed Fried Chicken

Medium-sized chicken	*1*	*Turmeric powder*	*½ tsp.*
Onions (big)	*2*	*Aniseed*	*½ tsp.*
Green chillies	*2*	*Garam masala powder*	*½ tsp.*
Ginger paste	*1 tsp.*	*Chopped cashewnuts*	*2 tbsp.*
Garlic paste	*1 tsp.*	*Raisins*	*1 tbsp.*
Coriander powder	*½ tsp.*	*Bengal gram dal*	*½ cup*
Chilli powder	*¼ tsp.*	*Hard-boiled egg*	*1*
Coriander leaves	*½ bunch*	*Salt*	*to taste*
Oil	*2 tbsp.*		

Batter

Egg	*1*	*Salt and chilli powder*	*to taste*
Maida	*1 tbsp.*	*Oil*	*for frying*

Clean the chicken and keep it whole. Wash the inside thoroughly. Cook the dal with coriander powder, ¼ tsp. turmeric powder and salt. Slice the onions and chillies. Chop the coriander leaves. Grind the aniseed.

Heat the oil. Add the onions and chillies and saute. Add the ginger and garlic paste. Fry till the onions are transparent. Add the cooked dal, cashewnuts, raisins, coriander leaves and garam masala powder. Fry for few seconds more. Remove from the fire. Stuff the chicken and masala and a whole hard-boiled egg. Push the legs through the tail end and stitch the legs together.

To 2 cups of water, add ¼ tsp. turmeric powder, chilli powder, aniseed paste and salt. Bring to boil. Add stuffed chicken. Cover and cook on a slow fire till done. Turn the chicken occassionally. Remove when done.

Make a batter with egg, maida, chilli powder and salt.

Smear the batter all over the chicken. Deep fry in hot oil to a golden brown. Take off the stitches and serve.

FISH

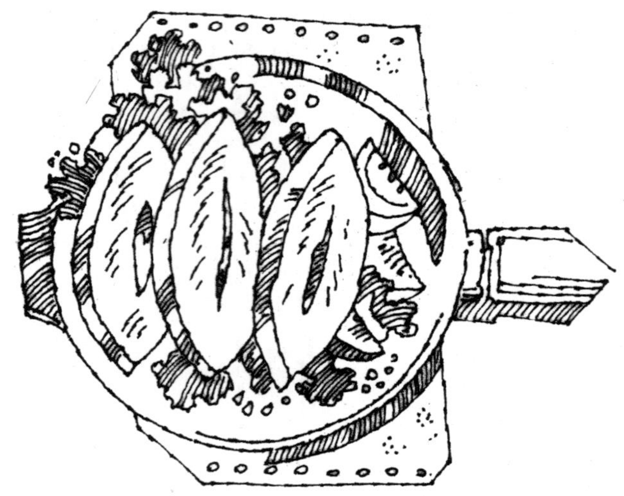

45. Meen Porichathu

(Fried Fish)

Fish (any fish)	*200 gm.*	*Cinnamon*	*4 cm. piece*
Chilli powder	*2 tsp.*	*Cloves*	*2*
Turmeric powder	*½ tsp.*	*Salt*	*to taste*
Aniseed	*1 tsp.*	*Oil*	*for frying*
Garlic	*4 cloves*		

Method

Clean, cut and wash the fish. Grind all the ingredients together to a paste. Apply to the fish and put it aside for some time.

Shallow fry in oil and remove.

46. Chemeen Porichathu

(Fried Prawns)

Shelled prawns	*200 gm.*	*Turmeric powder*	*½ tsp.*
Chilli powder	*3 tsp.*	*Aniseed*	*½ tsp.*
Garlic	*4 cloves*	*Salt*	*to taste*
Cinnamon	*4 cm. piece*	*Oil*	*for frying*
Cloves	*2*		

Clean and wash the prawns with a little salt. Grind all the ingredients with salt. Cook the prawns with ground ingredients in a little water till the prawns are cooked and the water absorbed.

Heat the oil in a kadai. Add the prawns and fry till the prawns are crisp.

47. Chemeen Manga Charu

(Prawn and Raw Mango Curry)

Shelled prawns	*200 gm.*	*Coriander powder*	*2 tbsp.*
Coconut	*½*	*Chilli powder*	*1 tsp.*
Raw mango	*1*	*Turmeric powder*	*½ tsp.*
Chopped onions (small)	*6*	*Aniseed*	*1 tsp.*
Onion (big)	*1*	*Fenugreek*	*1 tsp.*
Green chillies	*4*	*Mustard seed*	*½ tsp.*
Garlic	*½ pod*	*Curry leaves*	*2 sprigs*
Ginger	*2 cm. piece*	*Coconut oil*	*2 tbsp.*

Clean and remove the intestines of the prawns. Rub with a little salt and wash well. Slice the big onion, chillies and mango. Crush the ginger and garlic. Roast the coconut to a golden brown in 1/2 tsp. oil with the chopped small onion and aniseed, then grind to a smooth paste.

Heat the oil. Add the onion and green chillies. Fry till the onion is transparent. Add the green chillies, ginger and garlic. Fry for few seconds more. Add the chilli powder, coriander powder, turmeric powder and mango. Stir well and add 1 cup water. Add prawns and salt. Cook till the prawns are done. Mix ground coconut in 1 cup water and add to the curry. Boil and remove from the fire. Season with mustard, fenugreek and curry leaves.

48. Chemeen Cutlet

(Prawn Cutlet)

Shelled prawns	*200 gm.*	*Ginger*	*2 cm. piece*
Egg	*1*	*Chilli powder*	*1/2 tsp.*
Potatoes	*100 gm.*	*Turmeric powder*	*1/4 tsp.*
Onion (big)	*1*	*Oil*	*for frying*
Green chillies	*4*	*Coriander leaves*	*1/2 bunch*

Clean and remove the intestines of the prawns. Rub with little salt and wash. Cook prawns in a little water with chilli powder, turmeric powder and salt. Chop the onion, chillies, ginger and coriander leaves. Cook and mash the potatoes. Grind the prawns. Heat 1 tbsp. oil. Add the onion, chillies and ginger. Fry for a few seconds. Add the prawns and coriander leaves. Fry for a few seconds and remove from the fire. Add the mashed potato and egg. Mix well. Take small balls and shape into rounds. Shallow fry to a golden brown.

49. Meen Charu

(Fish Curry)

Mackerel or any other fish	*4*	*Fenugreek*	*½ tsp.*
Onions (small)	*8*	*Raw mango*	*1*
Green chillies	*4*	*Coconut*	*½*
Garlic	*4 cloves*	*Aniseed*	*½ tsp.*
Turmeric powder	*½ tsp.*	*Curry leaves*	*2 sprigs*
Chilli powder	*2 tsp.*	*Oil*	*2 tsp.*
Mustard seeds	*½ tsp.*	*Salt*	*to taste.*

Clean and remove the head of the mackerel and cut into two and wash. Slice the onion and green chillies. Grind the coconut to a smooth paste with aniseed and garlic. Cut the mango into long pieces.

Heat the oil. Add the mustard. When it crackles, add the fenugreek, onion and green chillies. Fry till the onion is lightly browned. Add 1 cup water, mango and all the powders. Boil for a few minutes. Add the fish and salt. Cook till the fish is done. Mix ground coconut with 1 cup water and add to the curry. Add curry leaves. Simmer and remove from the fire.

50. Meen Varatharacha Charu

(Fish in Coconut Gravy)

Seer fish or any other fish	*250 gm.*	*Chilli powder*	*2 tsp.*
Coconut	*½*	*Turmeric powder*	*½ tsp.*
Onion (big)	*1*	*Coriander powder*	*2 tbsp.*
		Aniseed	*1 tsp.*

Green chillies	*4*	*Big tomato*	*1*
Ginger	*2 cm. piece*	*Tamarind*	*small ball*
Garlic	*½ pod*	*Fenugreek*	*½ tsp.*
Chopped onion (small)	*1 tbsp.*	*Coriander leaves*	*½ bunch*
Curry leaves	*1 sprig*	*Salt*	*to taste*
Oil	*2 tbsp.*		

Clean and cut the fish into big slices and wash well. Slice the onion and chillies. Crush the ginger and garlic. Cut the tomato into four. Soak the tamarind in a little water. Roast coconut with aniseed, chopped small onion and few curry leaves in one tsp. oil to a golden brown and grind to a smooth paste.

Heat the oil. Add fenugreek. When it turns brown add the onion and chillies and saute. Add the ginger and garlic paste. Fry for few minutes. Add the tamarind water, chilli powder, coriander powder, turmeric powder and salt. Boil for few minutes. Add the fish and tomato. Cook till the fish is done. Mix the ground coconut in one cup water and add to the curry. Add coriander leaves and curry leaves. Simmer and remove from the fire.

51. Meen Varattiyathu

(Fish Masala)

Fish	*250 gm.*	*Chilli powder*	*1 tbsp.*
Onions (small)	*8*	*Fenugreek*	*1 tsp.*
Green chillies	*4*	*Mustard seeds*	*½ tsp.*
Garlic	*½ pod*	*Tamarind*	*small ball*
Ginger	*2 cm. piece*	*Curry leaves*	*2 sprigs*

Tomato	*1*	*Oil*	*2 tbsp.*
Turmeric powder	*½ tsp.*	*Salt*	*to taste*

Clean and cut the fish into big slices and wash. Chop the onion and chillies. Crush the ginger and garlic. Soak tamarind in a little water and squeeze out the juice. Cut the tomatoes into four.

Heat the oil. Add mustard. When it crackles add the fenugreek, onions, ginger and garlic. Fry till the onion is lightly browned. Add the tamarind water, chilli powder, turmeric powder and salt. Cook for a few minutes. Add the fish, tomatoes and curry leaves. Cook on a low heat till the fish is done and gravy thickens. Shake the pan occasionally to prevent burning.

52. Meen Kakkathilakkiyathu

(Fish Masala)

Fish	*250 gm.*	*Chilli powder*	*2 tbsp.*
Onions (big)	*2*	*Turmeric powder*	*½ tsp.*
Green chillies	*4*	*Garam masala powder*	*½ tsp.*
Garlic	*1 pod*	*Coriander leaves*	*½ bunch*
Ginger	*4 cm. piece*	*Oil*	*4 tbsp.*
Tomatoes (big)	*2*	*Salt*	*to taste*
Coriander powder	*2 tbsp.*	*Oil*	*for frying*

Clean and cut the fish into slices and wash. Apply a little

chilli powder, turmeric powder and salt to keep aside for a few minutes. Fry till lightly browned. Remove and keep aside. Slice the onion finely. Cut the tomatoes. Grind the ginger, garlic and green chilli separately. Chop the coriander leaves.

Heat 4 tbsp. oil. (If any oil is left over after this, use the same oil for frying). Add half the onion and fry till golden brown and remove. Crush and keep aside. Add the remaining onion and fry till transparent. Add the ground ingredients and fry till the aroma comes. Add all the powders, tomatoes, salt and 1 cup of water. Cook till the gravy is thick. Add the fish pieces and crushed onion. Cook on a low heat, shaking the pan occasionally. Cook till the oil oozes out. Add coriander leaves and garam masala powder. Remove from the fire.

53. Meen Mulakittathu

(Chilli-hot Fish Curry)

Mackerel or sardines	*4*	*Tamarind*	*small ball*
Onions (small)	*6*	*Mustard*	*½tsp.*
Green chillies	*2*	*Fenugreek*	*1 tsp.*
Garlic	*6 cloves*	*Coconut oil*	*2 tbsp.*
Tomato (big)	*1*	*Curry leaves*	*2 sprigs*
Chilli powder	*2 tbsp.*	*Salt*	*to taste*
Turmeric powder	*½ tsp.*		

Clean and remove the heads of the fish and wash well.

Chop the onion and green chillies. Crush the garlic. Soak the tamarind in a little water and squeeze out the juice. Cut the tomato into four. Heat the oil. Add mustard. When it starts to crackle, add the fenugreek, onion, green chillies and garlic. Fry for a few seconds. Add chilli powder, turmeric powder and tamarind water. Simmer for a few minutes. Add the fish, curry leaves and salt. Cook till the fish is done.

54. Mathi Nellikka Varattiyathu

(Sardines with Gooseberries)

Medium-sized sardines	*6*
Gooseberries (dried)	*2 tbsp.*
Pepper	*1 tbsp.*
Garlic	*6 cloves*
Fenugreek	*1 tsp.*
Coconut oil	*2 tbsp.*
Curry leaves	*few sprigs*

Clean and remove the heads of sardines, keeping them whole. Wash well. Remove seeds from the gooseberries and soak in water for some time. Grind them with pepper to a smooth paste. Crush the garlic.

Heat the oil. Add the fenugreek and when it becomes light brown add the garlic, ground pepper and gooseberry mixture. Fry for few seconds. Add 1 cup water, curry leaves and salt to taste. Simmer for a few minutes. Add the sardines. Cook on a low fire till the fish is done. Shake the pan occasionally to prevent burning. Cook till the gravy is almost dry.

55. Ayila Vattichathu

(Mackerel in Coconut Gravy)

Mackerel	*4*	*Turmeric powder*	*1/2 tsp.*
Coconut	*1/2*	*Aniseed*	*1 tsp.*
Onions (small)	*8*	*Mustard seeds*	*1/4 tsp.*
Green chillies	*4*	*Fenugreek*	*1/2 tsp.*
Tomatoes (big)	*2*	*Oil*	*2 tbsp.*
Garlic	*4 cloves*	*Curry leaves*	*2 sprigs*
Chilli powder	*3 tsp.*		

Clean and remove the heads of the mackerel and cut into two. Wash well. Slice the onion, chillies and tomatoes. Grind coconut to a coarse paste with aniseed and garlic.

Heat oil. Add mustard. When it starts to crackle add fenugreek, onion and green chillies. Fry till the onion is lightly browned. Add the tomatoes, chilli powder and turmeric powder. Stir well and add 1 cup water and salt. Cook for few minutes. Add fish and cook till the fish is done. Mix ground coconut in half cup water and add to the fish. Add the curry leaves. Simmer till the gravy is thick. Remove from the fire.

56. Ayila Puzungiyathu

Mackerel	*4*	*Ginger*	*2 cm. piece*
Onion (big)	*1*	*Coconut*	*1/2*
Green chillies	*6*	*Fenugreek*	*1/2 tsp.*
Tomato (big)	*1*	*Mustard seeds*	*1/2 tsp.*

Red chillies	*2*	*Curry leaves*	*2 sprigs*
Garlic	*6 cloves*	*Coconut oil*	*2 sprigs*

Clean and remove the head of the mackerel and cut into two. Wash head and pieces well. Chop the onion and green chillies. Crush the ginger and garlic. Cut the tomatoes into four. Crush the coconut and take ½ cup first milk and 1 cup second milk.

Heat the oil. Add the onion and green chillies. Fry for a few seconds. Add the tomatoes and second milk. When it boils, add the fish and salt. Cook till the fish is done. Add the first milk. Simmer; remove from fire. Temper with mustard, fenugreek, red chillies and curry leaves.

VEGETABLES

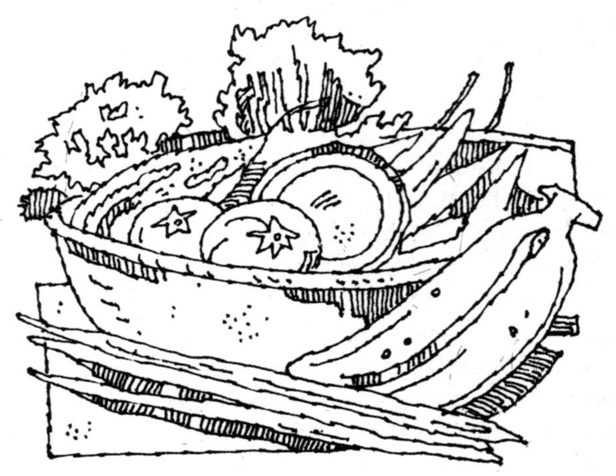

57. Vegetable Stew

Potatoes	*115 gm.*	*Ginger paste*	*½ tsp.*
Tomatoes	*115 gm.*	*Garlic paste*	*½ tsp.*
Carrots	*115 gm.*	*Coconut*	*½*
Beans	*100 gm.*	*Coriander leaves*	*½ bunch*
Onions	*100 gm.*	*Oil*	*2 tbsp.*
Green chillies	*6*	*Salt*	*to taste*

Wash and cut the vegetables. Slice the onion and green chillies. Grate the coconut and extract one cup first milk and one cup second milk.

Heat the oil. Add the onion and green chillies and fry till the onions are transparent. Add the ginger and garlic pastes, vegetables and salt. Fry for a few seconds. Add the second milk and cook till the vegetables are done.

Add the first milk. Simmer and remove from the fire. Add chopped coriander leaves.

58. Vegetable Khorma 1

Potatoes	*115 gm.*	*Garlic paste*	*1 tsp.*
Carrots	*115 gm.*	*Chilli powder*	*½tsp.*
Tomatoes	*115 gm.*	*Coriander powder*	*1 tsp.*
Beans	*100 gm.*	*Aniseed*	*1 tsp.*
Peas	*115 gm.*	*Cinnamon*	*4 cm. piece*
Onions	*115 gm.*	*Cardamoms*	*3*
Green chillies	*4*	*Cloves*	*3*
Coconut	*½*	*Coriander leaves*	*½ bunch*
Ginger paste	*1 tsp.*	*Salt*	*to taste*

Wash and cut the vegetables. Slice the onions and chillies. Grind the coconut, aniseed, cloves, cardamom and cinnamon together to a smooth paste.

Heat the oil. Add the onion and green chillies and fry. Fry till the onions are lightly browned. Add the ginger-garlic paste and all the vegetables. Fry for a few seconds. Add the chilli powder and coriander powder. Stir well and add one cup water. Add salt to taste. Cook till the vegetables are done. Mix the ground coconut with a little water and add to the vegetables. Add chopped coriander leaves. Simmer and remove from the fire.

59. Vegetable Khorma 2

Potatoes	*115 gm.*	*Ginger paste*	*1 tsp.*

Carrots	*115 gm.*	*Chilli powder*	*1 tsp.*
Peas	*115 gm.*	*Turmeric powder*	*1/2 tsp.*
Tomatoes	*115 gm.*	*Coriander powder*	*2 tsp.*
Onions	*115 gm.*	*Poppy seeds*	*1/2 tsp.*
Green chillies	*4*	*Curd*	*1/2 cup*
Garlic paste	*1 tsp.*	*Grated coconut*	*1 cup*
Cloves	*3*	*Oil*	*2 tbsp.*
Cardamoms	*3*	*Aniseed*	*1 tsp.*
Cinnamon	*4 cm. piece*	*Salt*	*to taste*
Coriander leaves	*1/2 bunch*		

Wash and cut the vegetables. Slice the onions. Grind the coconut with aniseed, cloves, cardamom and cinnamon to a smooth paste. Grind the poppy seeds separately.

Heat the oil. Add the onions and fry till transparent. Add the ginger-garlic paste and all the vegetables. Fry for a few seconds. Add coriander powder, chilli powder, turmeric powder and ground poppy seeds. Stir well. Add curd, salt and just enough water to cook the vegetables. When the vegetables are cooked add the ground coconut mixed with a little water. Add chopped coriander leaves. Simmer and remove from the fire.

60. Chena Charu

(Yam Curry)

Yam	*200 gm.*	*Aniseed*	*1 tsp.*
Coconut	*1/2*	*Mustard seed*	*1/4 tsp.*
Chilli powder	*1 tsp.*	*Curry leaves*	*1 sprig*
Turmeric powder	*1/2 tsp.*	*Oil*	*1 tbsp.*
Coriander powder	*1 tbsp.*	*Salt*	*to taste*
Chopped onion (small)	*1 tbsp.*		

Peel and cut the yam into big pieces and wash. Cook the yam with coriander powder, chilli powder and turmeric powder.

Heat 1 tsp. oil in a kadai and roast the coconut with aniseed to a golden brown. Remove from the fire and grind to a smooth paste. Mix with a little water and add to the cooked yam. Add salt to taste. Heat the remaining oil. Add mustard. When it crackles add the chopped onion. Fry the onion to a golden brown. Pour it onto the curry. Add curry leaves. Simmer and remove from the fire.

61. Thakkali Vattichathu

(Tomato Masala)

Tomatoes	*250 gm.*	*Garlic*	*4 cloves*
Onion (big)	*1*	*Aniseed*	*1 tsp.*
Green chillies	*4*	*Mustard seeds*	*1/4 tsp.*
Coconut	*1/2*	*Curry leaves*	*1 sprig*
Chilli powder	*1 tsp.*	*Oil*	*1 tbsp.*
Turmeric powder	*1/2 tsp.*	*Salt*	*to taste*

Wash and slice the tomatoes. Chop the onion and green chillies. Grind the coconut with aniseed and garlic to a coarse paste. Heat the oil and add mustard. When it crackles add the onion and green chillies. Fry for a few seconds. Add the tomatoes, chilli powder and turmeric powder. Fry for a few seconds more. Add a little water and salt. When the tomatoes are cooked add the ground coconut and curry leaves. Simmer and remove from the fire.

62. Thakkali Mulakittathu

(Hot Tomato Curry)

Tomatoes	*250 gm.*	*Cloves garlic*	*4*
Onion (big)	*1*	*Mustard seeds*	*¼ tsp.*
Green chillies	*3*	*Oil*	*2 tbsp.*
Chilli powder	*2 tsp.*	*Salt*	*to taste*
Turmeric powder	*½ tsp.*		

Wash and slice the tomatoes, onion and green chillies. Crush the garlic.

Heat the oil. Add mustard. When it starts to crackle, add the onion and green chillies and fry till the onions are transparent. Add the garlic, tomatoes, chilli powder, turmeric powder and salt. Stir well and add 1 cup water. Cook till the tomatoes are done.

63. Vendakka Mulakittathu

(Hot Lady's Finger Curry)

Lady's fingers	*200 gm.*	*Tamarind*	*small ball (the size of a small lime)*
Green chillies	*2*	*Mustard seed*	*¼ tsp.*
Onion (big)	*1*	*Curry leaves*	*1 sprig*
Tomatoes	*100 gm.*	*Oil*	*2 tsp.*
Chilli powder	*2 tsp.*	*Salt*	*to taste*
Turmeric powder	*½ tsp.*		
Garlic	*4 cloves*		

Wash and cut the lady's fingers into thin, round pieces. Chop the tomatoes, onion and green chillies. Crush the garlic. Soak the tamarind in a little water and squeeze out juice.

Heat the oil. Add the lady's fingers and onion. Fry till lightly browned. Add all the other ingredients except tamarind and mustard. Fry for 2-3 minutes. Add the tamarind water and salt. Cook till the lady's fingers are done. Temper with mustard and curry leaves.

64. Parippu Thalichathu

(Coconut Dal)

Thur dal	*1 cup*	*Aniseed*	*1 tsp.*
Coconut	*½*	*Mustard seeds*	*½ tsp.*
Chilli powder	*½ tsp.*	*Curry leaves*	*1 sprig*
Turmeric powder	*¼ tsp.*	*Oil*	*2 tsp.*
Garlic	*4 cloves*	*Salt*	*to taste*

Cook dal with chilli powder, turmeric powder and salt. Grind coconut to a smooth paste with aniseed and garlic. Add to the cooked dal. Temper with mustard and curry leaves.

65. Muringayila Thalichathu

(Drumstick-leaf Curry)

Drumstick leaves	*1 handful*	*Aniseed*	*½ tsp.*
		Garlic	*4 cloves*
Coconut	*½*	*Mustard seeds*	*¼ tsp.*
Onion (big)	*1*	*Oil*	*1 tbsp.*

Green chillies	*3*	*Curry leaves*	*1 sprig*
Chilli powder	*1 tbsp.*	*Salt*	*to taste*
Turmeric powder	*1/4 tsp.*		

Wash the drumstick leaves. Chop the onion and green chillies. Grind coconut to a smooth paste with aniseed, garlic and turmeric powder.

Heat the oil. Add mustard. When it crackles add the onion and green chillies. Fry for a while. Add the drumstick leaves and fry for few seconds more. Add the chilli powder and ground coconut mixed with 1 1/2 cups of water. Add the curry leaves and salt. Simmer and remove from the fire.

66. Muringayila Ulathiyathu

(Drumstick-leaf Masala)

Drumstick leaves	*2 handfuls*	*Aniseed*	*1 tsp.*
Coconut	*1/2*	*Garlic*	*4 cloves*
Red chillies	*4*	*Mustard seeds*	*1/4 tsp.*
Turmeric powder	*1/4 tsp.*	*Oil*	*1 tbsp.*
		Salt	*to taste*

Grind the coconut to a coarse paste with the red chilli, aniseed, turmeric powder, garlic and salt.

Heat the oil. Add mustard. When it crackles add the drumstick leaves. Fry till the leaves are lightly transparent. Add the coconut paste and stir well. Sprinkle a little water. Cover and cook till the water is absorbed.

67. Kayippakka Vartharacha Curry

(Bitter Gourd in Coconut Gravy)

Bitter gourds (small)	*3*	*Coriander seed*	*2 tsp.*
Coconut	*½*	*Turmeric*	*1 cm. piece*
Red chillies	*6*	*Aniseed*	*1 tsp.*
Onions (small)	*6*	*Tamarind*	*small ball*
Green chillies	*4*	*Oil*	*2 tsp.*
Onion (big)	*1*	*Mustard seed*	*a little*
Garlic	*4 cloves*	*Curry leaves*	*few sprigs*
Cumminseed	*½ tsp.*	*Salt*	*to taste*

Wash and cut the bitter gourds into thin, long slices. Roast and grind the red chillies, coriander seed and turmeric together. Roast the coconut with the cumminseed and aniseed and half of the small onion. Grind to a smooth paste with garlic. Slice the remaining onion and green chillies. Soak tamarind in a little water and squeeze out the juice. Parboil the bitter gourd and strain off the water.

Heat the oil. Add the onion and green chillies and fry for a minute. Add the ground coriander and chilli paste and fry for few seconds more. Add the bitter gourd and 1 cup water and salt to taste and cook. Add the tamarind water. Cook for few minutes more. Mix the ground coconut in a cup of water and add to the curry. Simmer and remove from the fire. Heat the remaining 1 tbsp. oil and fry mustard and curry leaves. Add this to the prepared curry.

68. Kayippakka Mulakittathu

(Hot Bitter-gourd Curry)

Bitter gourds (small)	*3*	*Tomato (big)*	*1*

Chopped onion (small)	*2 tbsp.*	*Tamarind*	*small ball*
Green chillies	*2*	*Oil*	*1 tbsp.*
Chilli powder	*2 tsp.*	*Mustard seeds and curry leaves for tempering*	
Turmeric powder	*1/4 tsp.*		

Wash and cut the bitter gourds into thin, round slices. Slice the tomato and green chillies. Soak the tamarind in a little water and squeeze out the juice.

Heat the oil. Add the chopped onion, chillies and bitter gourd and fry till the bitter gourd is lightly browned. Add the tomato, chilli powder, turmeric powder and one cup water. When the bitter gourd is half done add tamarind water and salt. Cook till done. Temper with mustard and curry leaves.

69. Kaya Upperi

(Banana Dry Curry)

Raw Malabar bananas or any other variety	*2*	*Oil*	*2 tsp.*
Red chillies	*4*	*Mustard seeds and curry leaves for seasoning*	
Turmeric powder	*1/2 tsp.*		

Peel and cut the bananas lengthwise and chop into small pieces. Wash well with a little salt. Cook with turmeric powder till soft and the water is absorbed. Add salt. Cut the red chillies into two. Heat the oil. Add mustard. When it crackles add the chillies and curry leaves. Add to the cooked bananas and stir well.

70. Kaya Puzungiyathu

(Banana and Coconut Curry)

Malabar bananas (half ripened)	*2*	*Chilli powder*	*1 tsp.*
Grated coconut	*1 cup*	*Turmeric powder*	*½ tsp.*
Aniseed	*½ tsp.*	*Curry leaves*	*2 sprigs*
Garlic	*2 cloves*	*Salt*	*to taste*

Peel and cut the bananas, first lengthwise, then slantwise into 2-inch long pieces. Wash well with a little salt. Cook with chilli powder and turmeric powder till soft. Add salt.

Grind the coconut to a smooth paste with aniseed and garlic. Mix it with a little water and add to the cooked bananas. Add curry leaves and simmer for few minutes. Remove from the fire.

Note. This curry goes well with Neichoru.

71. Manga Charu

(Raw Mango Curry)

Raw mangoes (big)	*2*	*Oil*	*2 tsp.*
Coconut	*½*	*Mustard seeds*	*¼ tsp.*
Chilli powder	*1 tsp.*	*Water*	*1 cup*
Turmeric powder	*½ tsp.*	*Curry leaves*	*few sprigs*
Garlic	*4 cloves*	*Salt*	*to taste*

Wash and cut the mangoes into big pieces without peeling them. Grind the coconut to a smooth paste with garlic.

Heat the oil. Add mustard and when it starts to crackle

add the chilli powder, turmeric powder, mango pieces, salt and 1 cup water. Cover and cook till the mango pieces are soft. Mix the ground coconut with a little water and add to the cooked mango. Add curry leaves. Simmer and remove from the fire.

72. Kadu Manga

(Mango Curry with Mustard)

Raw mangoes	*2*	*Mustard seeds*	*½ tsp.*
Chilli powder	*2 tsp.*	*Oil*	*1 tbsp.*
Turmeric powder	*¼ tsp.*	*Water*	*1 cup*
Garlic	*4 cloves*	*Salt*	*to taste*

Wash and cut the mango into big pieces without removing the peel. Crush garlic.

Heat the oil. Add the mustard and when it starts to crackle add the garlic and fry for a while. Add the chilli powder, turmeric powder, mango pieces, salt and 1 cup water. Cover and cook till the mango pieces are soft.

73. Chakkara Kadu Manga

(Sweet and Sour Mango)

Half-ripened mangoes	*2*	*Oil*	*1 tbsp.*
Jaggery	*50 gm.*	*Mustard*	*½ tsp.*
Whole red chillies	*4 to 5*	*Water*	*2 cups*

Garlic	*4 cloves*	*Salt*	*to taste*

Wash and cut the mango into long, thick pieces without removing the peel. Grind the chillies with garlic.

Heat the oil. Add mustard and when it crackles add the chilli and garlic paste and stir well for a second. Add 2 cups water and mango pieces. When the mango pieces are half done add jaggery and salt to taste. Cook till the pieces are soft and the gravy thickens. Remove from the fire.

EGGS

74. Mutta Curry

(Egg Curry)

Eggs	*2*	*Garlic*	*4 cloves*
Coconut	*½*	*Oil*	*2 tbsp.*
Green chillies (chopped)	*4*	*Curry leaves*	*1 sprig*
Chopped onion (small)	*2 tbsp.*	*Water*	*1 ½ cups*
Chilli powder	*1 tsp.*	*Salt*	*to taste*
Aniseed	*½ tsp.*		

Grind the coconut to a smooth paste with aniseed and garlic. Heat the oil and saute onion and chillies. Add the chilli powder, turmeric powder and ground coconut mixed in 1½ cups water. Add salt and curry leaves.

Simmer for a few minutes. If it is too thick add a little more water. Reduce the heat and break the eggs and stir well till the egg is done. Remove immediately from the fire; otherwise the curry may curdle.

75. Mutta Omelette Curry

(Egg-Omelette Curry)

Eggs	*4*	*Turmeric powder*	*1/4 tsp.*
Onion (big)	*1*	*Grated coconut*	*2 tbsp.*
Green chillies	*2*	*Oil*	*2 tsp.*
Chilli powder	*1/2 tsp.*	*Salt*	*to taste*

For the Gravy

Onion (big)	*1*	*Coconut*	*1/2*
Green chillies	*2*	*Tomatoes (big)*	*2*
Ginger paste	*1/2 tsp.*	*Coriander leaves*	*1/2 bunch*
Garlic paste	*1/2 tsp.*	*Oil*	*3 tbsp.*
Coriander seeds	*1 tbsp.*	*Water*	*1 cup*
Chilli powder	*1 1/2 tsp.*	*Salt*	*to taste*
Turmeric powder	*1/2 tsp.*		

Chop the onions and green chillies. Beat the eggs and add all the ingredients except oil. Heat 1 tsp. oil in a frying pan. Using half the egg mixture each time, make two omelettes. Do not overcook. Cut the omelettes into 2-inch slices. Keep aside.

Gravy

Chop the onions, green chillies, tomatoes and coriander

leaves. Roast the coriander seeds without oil and remove. Heat 1 tsp. oil and roast the coconut to a golden colour. Grind the coriander seeds and coconut separately.

Heat the oil and saute onion and green chillies. Add the ginger-garlic paste and fry for a few seconds. Add the coriander paste, chilli powder, turmeric powder, tomatoes, salt and 1 cup water. Simmer for five minutes. Mix the ground coconut in 1 cup water and add to the curry and boil. Add omelette slices and boil for a few seconds more. Add coriander leaves and remove from fire. If the curry is too thick dilute with a little hot water.

76. Mutta Kakkathilakkiyathu

(Egg Masala)

Hard-boiled eggs	*4*	*Garlic*	*4 cloves*
Onion (big)	*1*	*Aniseed*	*2 tsp.*
Tomatoes	*2*	*Oil*	*50 ml.*
Chilli powder	*2 tsp.*	*Water*	*½ cup*
Turmeric powder	*½ tsp.*	*Salt*	*to taste*

Grind the aniseed and garlic with chilli powder and turmeric powder. Chop the onion and tomatoes.

Heat the oil and fry onion till lightly browned. Add the ground masala and fry a few seconds. Add the tomatoes and ½cup water and salt to taste. Cook till the gravy is thick. Add the egg and cook till the oil oozes out. Remove from fire.

77. Mutta Ulathiyathu

(Scrambled Egg)

Eggs	*3*	*Coconut*	*1/2*
Onion (big)	*1*	*Oil*	*1 tbsp.*
Green chillies	*4*	*Curry leaves*	*2 sprigs*
Chilli powder	*1 tsp.*	*Water*	*1/2 cup*
Turmeric powder	*1/2 tsp.*	*Salt*	*to taste*
Aniseed	*1 tsp.*		

Grind the aniseed. Add the coconut, chilli powder and turmeric powder and grind coarsely. Chop the onion and green chillies. Beat the eggs with salt.

Heat the oil and saute onion and green chillies. Add the ground coconut masala and stir well. Add 1/2 cup water, salt and curry leaves. When the water is absorbed add the beaten egg and stir well till the eggs are done.

78. Mutta Porichathu

(Fried Eggs)

Eggs	*4*	*Turmeric powder*	*1/2tsp.*
Green chillies	*2*	*Oil*	*2 tbsp.*
Onions (big)	*2*	*Curry leaves*	*1 sprig*
Grated coconut	*1 cup*	*Salt*	*to taste*

Chop onions and green chillies. Beat eggs and add all the ingredients except oil.

Heat 1 tbsp. oil in a kadai or frying pan. Pour in half of the egg mixture. Do not spread, but allow it to remain thick. Keep on a low fire till the bottom is cooked. Turn it over and cook the other side. Cook till both sides are golden brown and remove. Cook the rest of the egg in the same way.

79. Masala Egg

Hard boiled eggs	*4*
Turmeric powder	*1/2 tsp.*
Cloves garlic	
Oil	*for frying*
Turmeric powder	*1/2 tsp.*
Chilli powder	*1 tsp.*
Salt	*to taste*

Grind the aniseed, chilli powder, turmeric powder, garlic and salt. Shell the eggs and make four slight slits in the egg without breaking it. Apply the ground masala all over the egg and keep it aside for few minutes. Heat the oil and shallow fry the egg to a golden brown.

SWEETS, SWEET SNACKS AND PUDDINGS

80. Kari

(Banana and Coconut Pudding)

Ripe Malabar bananas	*5*	*Rice flour*	*2 tbsp.*
Sugar	*150 gm.*	*Cardamom (powdered)*	*4 pods*
Coconut	*1*		
Boiled rice	*200 gm.*		

Clean and soak the rice in cold water for 3-4 hours. Wash and drain the rice. Add salt and grind to a smooth paste. Oil your hands, take a little rice paste at a time, roll out thin, 2 cm. long pieces (pidi) with your hands. Arrange in a piece of banana leaf or cloth and steam till cooked. Remove from the vessel and sprinkle cold water over them and separate with the hands. Keep the *pidi* aside.

Peel and cut the bananas into two, lengthwise, and

cut into pieces slantwise. Grate and crush the coconut. Extract 2 cups first milk and 4 cups second milk. Add the banana pieces to the second milk and cook till the banana is soft. Add sugar, a pinch of salt and the steamed *pidi*. Cook for a few minutes more. Mix the rice flour with a little coconut milk (just milk) and add to the banana mixture. Keep on a low fire, stirring well till it thickens. Add the rest of the first milk. When it starts to boil remove from the fire. Sprinkle over with cardamom powder. Serve hot or cold.

81. Kadalakka Kari

(Rice Pudding)

Boiled rice	*100 gm.*	*Rice flour*	*2 tbsp.*
Sugar	*100 gm.*	*Cardamom (powdered)*	*5 pods*
Coconut	*1*	*Salt*	*to taste*
Bengal gram dal	*100 gm.*		

Wash and soak the dal in cold water for half an hour. Clean and soak the rice in cold water for 3 hours. Drain and grind the rice with salt to a smooth paste. Oil your hands and take a little rice paste at a time, roll it with your hands into a small pellet and then press it to form a small button. Steam the *pidi* till cooked. Remove and sprinkle over with a little cold water and separate with the fingers. Keep aside.

Grate and crush the coconut. Extract 1 cup milk and 2 cups second milk. Cook dal in 2 cups water till half cooked. Add second milk, steamed *pidi* and sugar. Cook till the dal is soft. Make a paste with rice flour and water.

Add to the dal. Keep on a low fire till the Kari is thick. Add a pinch of salt, add the first milk and cardamom powder. When it starts to boil remove from fire. Serve hot or cold.

82. Kaya Porichathu

(Banana Fritters)

Fully ripe bananas	*2*	*Rose water*	*1 tsp.*
Sugar	*1 tsp.*	*Ghee*	*for frying*

Peel and slice the bananas into thin long pieces. Heat the ghee. Fry the bananas golden brown, and remove. Sprinkle over with sugar and rose water.

83. Kaya Mukkiporichathu

(Fried Banana)

Fully ripe Malabar bananas	*2*	*Baking soda*	*a pinch*
Flour	*1 cup*	*Oil*	*for frying*
Sugar	*1 tbsp.*	*Water*	*a little*
Egg	*1*	*Salt*	*to taste*
Cardamom powder	*a pinch*		

Peel and cut the banana slantwise into thin pieces. Beat the egg and add sugar. Add maida and a little water and make a thin batter. Add cardamom powder, baking soda and a pinch of salt. Heat the oil. Dip the banana slices in the batter and deep fry to a golden brown. Remove and drain.

84. Unnakkayi

(Banana 'Cotton-Buds')

Half-ripe Malabar bananas	*2*	*Chopped cashewnuts*	*1 tbsp.*
Eggs	*2*	*Ghee*	*2 tsp.*
Sugar	*2 tbsp.*	*Oil*	*for frying*
Raisins	*1 tsp.*	*Cardamom powder*	*a little*

Cut the banana into two or three pieces and cook in boiling water till the peel separates slightly from the fruit. Remove from fire and strain. Remove the peel and grind the banana to a smooth dough without adding any water. Keep aside. Mix the eggs with sugar. Do not overbeat. Heat 2 tsp. ghee in a saucepan. Add the eggs mixture and stir it well till it reaches scrambled egg consistency. Remove from the fire. Add the cashewnuts, raisins and cardamom powder. Oil your hands and take small balls (the size of a lime) of the ground banana. Flatten on your palm into a small disc. Put 2 tsp. of scrambled egg in it. Fold the edges and press lightly. Now roll it with your hands, and shape it like cotton buds (both the ends pointed).

Heat oil and deep fry to a golden brown and remove. You will get about 6 unnakkayas.

85. Scrambled Banana

Ripe Malabar bananas	*2*	*Chopped cashewnuts*	*1 tbsp.*
Eggs	*2*	*Raisins*	*1 tbsp.*
Sugar	*1 tbsp.*	*Ghee*	*2 tbsp.*
Vanilla essence or cardamom powder for flavouring			

Cut the bananas into small pieces. Beat the eggs and sugar together. Heat the ghee and shallow-fry banana pieces to a golden brown. Add egg mixture and stir well. Add cashewnuts, raisins and essence. Stir till the egg is cooked. Remove from the fire.

86. Stuffed Banana

Ripe Malabar bananas	*2*	*Cardamom (powdered)*	*2 pods*
Sugar	*2 tbsp.*	*Flour*	*2 tbsp.*
Eggs	*2*	*Water*	*for mixing*
Raisins	*1 tbsp.*	*Oil*	*for frying*
Cashewnuts (chopped)	*2 tbsp.*		

Beat the eggs with sugar. Heat 1 tsp. ghee. Add the egg and stir well to scrambled-egg consistency. Add cashewnuts, raisins and cardamom powder. Remove from the fire. Peel the banana and slit it into four without cutting the ends. Stuff the banana with the scrambled eggs. Make a paste with flour and water. Apply the paste on the stuffing. Heat the oil and slowly put the banana in it. Deep fry to a golden brown and remove.

87. Banana in Syrup

Ripe bananas	*2*	*Raisins*	*1 tbsp.*
Sugar	*1 cup*	*Rose water*	*1 tbsp.*
Cashewnuts (chopped)	*1 tbsp.*	*Water*	*½ cup*

Cut the bananas into two. Cook in water till the skin separates slightly. Drain off the water and peel the fruit. Cut into thick round pieces. Add half cup water with sugar and make a thin syrup. Add the banana pieces and keep on the fire till the syrup thickens to a one-string consistency. Remove from the fire. Add the cashewnuts, raisins and rose water.

88. Ada

(Rice and Coconut Pie)

Boiled rice	*400 gm.*	*Salt*	*to taste*
Coconut	½		

For the Filling

Coconut	*1*	*Cardamom (powdered)*	*6 pods*
Jaggery	*200 gm.*	*Water*	*a little*

Clean and soak the rice in cold water for 3-4 hours, then wash and strain. Grate the coconut and mix with rice. Grind to a smooth paste with sufficient salt.

The Filling

Grate the coconut. Melt the jaggery with a little water. When melted, remove and strain. Add the coconut and cardamom powder. Stir and cook till the water dries up. Remove from the fire and keep aside.

Take small balls of rice paste and flatten onto a piece of banana leaf or cloth into small discs. Put 1 tbsp. of filling on one side and fold the other half over, pressing down the edge. Steam till cooked. Remove, cool and serve.

89. Kayada

(Rice and Banana Pie)

Bananas	*2 doz.*	*Coconut*	*½*
Jaggery	*250 gm.*	*Banana leaf*	*few pieces*
Raw rice	200 gm.		

Clean and soak the rice in cold water for 2 hours. Wash and drain. Pound to a fine powder, sieve and keep aside. Peel the banana and mash it up well till it is creamy. Grate the coconut. Melt the jaggery in a little water. Remove and strain. Add all the ingredients to the mashed banana and mix well. Wash and cut the banana leaf into 10-12 cm. wide pieces. Now fold the leaf into a cone shape (as for a samosa). Pour the banana mixture into the cone and fold down the end. Put the cones on the lid of the idli vessel with the folded edges facing downward and steam till cooked. Remove from vessel. Cool, remove leaves and serve.

90. Thari Choru

(Semolina Dessert)

Semolina	*100 gm.*	*Raisins*	*2 tbsp.*
Sugar	*100 gm.*	*Rose water*	*2 tsp.*
Ghee or dalda	*50 gm.*	*Water*	*1 cup*
Cashewnuts (chopped)	*2 tbsp.*		

Heat the ghee and fry the cashewnuts and raisins to a golden brown and remove. Add the semolina and fry for a few seconds. Mix sugar with 1 cup water and to semolina. Stir well and keep on a low fire till the moisture is absorbed. Add the fried cashewnuts and raisins.

Sprinkle rose water and remove from the fire.

91. Thari Unda

(Semolina Laddu)

Semolina	*200 gm.*	*Cashewnuts (chopped)*	*2 tbsp.*
Grated coconut	*½ cup*	*Rose water*	*1 tsp.*
Sugar	*200 gm.*	*Cardamom (powdered)*	*5 pods*
Raisins	*2 tbsp.*	*Water*	*½ cup*

Roast the semolina without oil, and cool. Add ½ cup water to sugar and make a sticky syrup. Add all the ingredients and stir well. Remove from the fire and form into even-sized balls.

Sweet Envelope

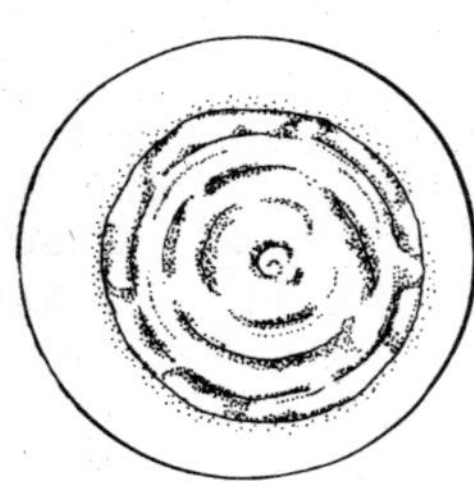

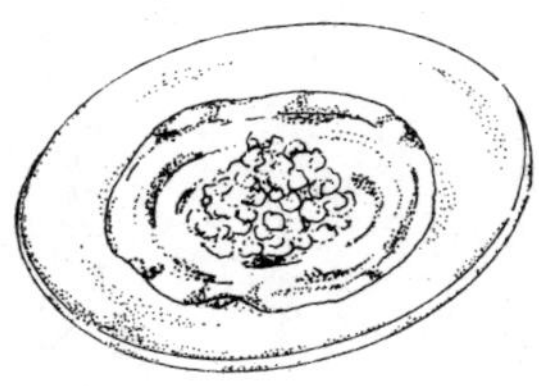

1. Make a round pancake, about six cm. in diameter. Fill with egg mixture.

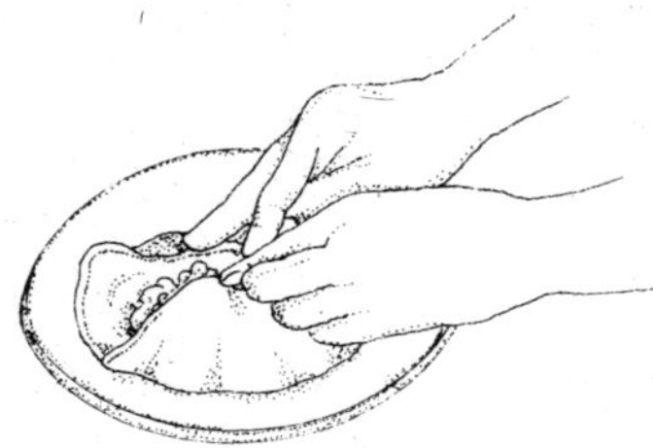

2. Fold the edges inwards on all sides to make an envelope shape. Seal the edges with batter and then place on a hot tava with the sealed edge down to make it firm.

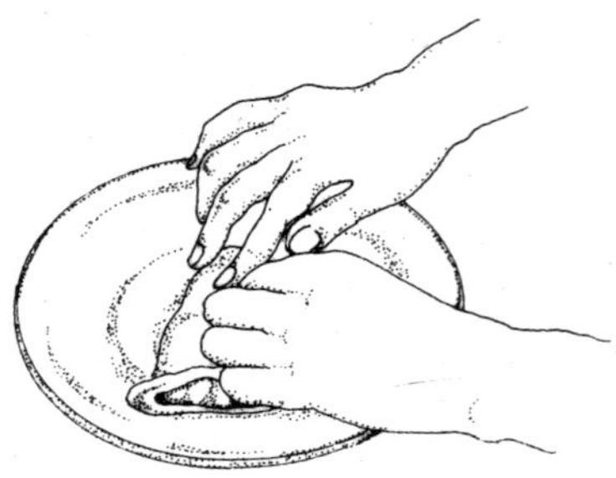

3. Repeat process with two more pancakes of successively larger diameters. Take care to see that the third one is large enough to accommodate the earlier two filled envelopes. Like this you will have two filled envelopes inside the largest, third envelope.

4. Place the largest envelope on a soup plate, pour syrup on top and garnish with raisins and cashewnuts.

92. Thariyappam

(Semolina Pancakes)

Semolina (1 cup)	*50 gm.*	*Cardamom, (powdered)*	*3 pods*
Eggs	*3*	*Ghee*	*for frying*
Sugar	*4 tbsp.*		

Beat the eggs and sugar till well mixed. Add semolina and cardamom powder. Heat a tava and pour a little ghee on it. Put a tablespoon of batter onto the tava, reduce heat and cook to a golden brown. You can cook 3-4 thariyappams at a time.

93. Sweet Envelope Appam

Flour	*1½ cups*	*Milk*	*½ cup*
Eggs	*5*	*Ghee*	*2 tbsp.*
Sugar	*1 cup*	*Rose water*	*a little*
Cashewnuts	*(2 tbsp.) 25 gm.*	*Water*	*a little*
Cardamom powder	*a pinch*	*Raisins*	*(2 tsp.) 25 gm.*
		Salt	*to taste*

Make a thin batter with the flour, one egg, milk and a little water. Add salt to taste. Beat the remaining three eggs with half cup sugar. Heat 1 tsp. ghee in a saucepan. Add the beaten eggs and stir well, cooking to scrambled egg consistency. Remove from the fire. Add half of the chopped cashewnuts and raisins and cardamom powder. Keep aside.

Heat a tava. Make a small pancake about 6 cm. in diameter. Dot with ghee and turn it over. When done remove on to a plate. Put a little egg filling in the middle of the pancake and fold to form an envelope. Keep it in the plate. Make a second pancake bigger than the first one. It should be big enough to cover the first filled pancake. When cooked remove to a plate and put some filling in the middle. Put the first folded pancake on the filling and fold the four edges as you did the first one. Seal the edges with a little batter and keep it on the tava with sealed edge down and press it a little to make it firm. Now make a third pancake bigger than the second and proceed as before. Make two more such envelope appams with the remaining batter and filling (3 in all).

Add 1 cup water to the remaining sugar and make a thin syrup. Sprinkle rose water and remove from fire. Place all the envelope appams in a big soup plate. Pour syrup over them. Garnish with raisins and cashewnuts.

94. Kalathappam

(Sweet Rice Cakes)

Raw rice	*400 gm.*	*Oil*	*2 tbsp.*
Jaggery	*500 gm.*	*Cardamom (powdered)*	*4 pods*
Chopped onions (small)	*4*	*Water*	*1 1/2 cups*

Pick, clean and soak rice in water for 2 hours. Wash and drain the rice and pound to a very fine powder and sieve it twice. Dissolve jaggery in 1 1/2 cups water and boil till it is thick. Strain and keep aside. When the syrup becomes lukewarm add rice flour and beat well with a wooden

Muttamala

1. Fill egg yolk in a coconut shell with a single hole at the bottom, stopping the hole with your finger.

2. Place the coconut shell above the boiling sugar syrup, remove your finger and allow the yolk to pour, moving your hand in a continuous circular motion, till all the yolk is used up.

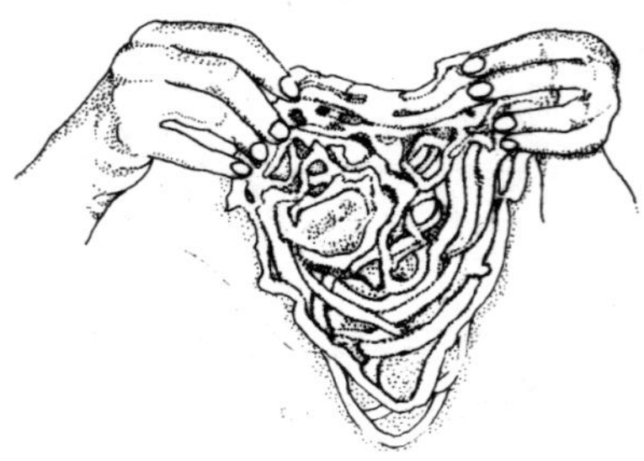

3. Remove the cooked egg yolk from the vessel gently with the help of two forks. See that the mala does not break.

4. Arrange the muttamala in a plate and garnish with egg snow pudding made with the egg whites. (See recipe for Pinnanathappam.)

masher or egg beater to make a pouring consistency. Add cardamom powder.

Heat oil in an *uruli* and fry onion to a light brown. Pour in the rice mixture and turn down the heat very low. Cover with a heavy lid and put some live coals on top and bake till done.

This can also be poured into a cake tin and baked in an oven.

95. Mutta Mala

(Egg-Yolk Garlands)

Eggs	*15*	*Water*	*3 cups*
Sugar	*500 gm.*		

Separate the yolks and whites of the egg. Keep the whites for Pinnanathappam (the following recipe). Strain the egg yolk through a muslin cloth into a clean dry bowl. Clean a coconut shell and make a very small hole at the bottom. Put sugar and 2 cups water in a wide heavy vessel (an *uruli*). Add a little egg white, rubbing it well. Place it on the fire. When it boils remove all the scum. Remove it from the fire and strain through a muslin cloth. Heat it again and make a syrup of one-string consistency.

Take the coconut shell and fill it with egg yolk, stopping the hole with your finger. Remove your finger and pour the yolk in the boiling syrup in a circular motion to form chain-like strings. Pour it continuously until the egg yolk in the shell has all been used up. By this time the yolk will be cooked. Reduce the heat and sprinkle a little cold water.

Remove the egg strings from the syrup without

breaking them. Spread in a thali and keep slightly raised to remove the excess syrup. Use up all the egg yolks this way. When the syrup becomes thick add a little water to bring it back to a one string consistency. Arrange the Mutta Mala in a large plate and put Pinnanathappam in the middle.

Note: The leftover syrup can be used for Pinnanathappam.

96. Pinnanathappam

(Egg Snow Pudding)

Egg whites	*15*	*Cardamom (powdered)*	*6 pods*
leftover syrup from Mutta Mala			

Beat the egg whites well. Cool the Mutta Mala syrup and add it to the egg white. Beat till frothy. Add cardamom powder. Heat water in an idli vessel. Grease a wide vessel and pour in the beaten egg white. Steam it in an idli vessel till firm. Remove and cool. Cut into diamond shaped pieces and serve with Mutta Mala.

97. Naiyada

(Baked Fruit and Nut Pudding)

Flour	*100 gm.*	*Cashewnuts*	*50 gm.*
Eggs	*4*	*Raisins*	*50 gm.*
Milk	*1 cup*	*Ghee*	*100 gm.*
Sugar	*150 gm.*	*Cardamom powder*	*a pinch*

Make a thin batter with the flour, milk and salt to taste. Add a little water if necessary. Beat the eggs well with sugar. Chop the cashewnuts. Take a small vessel or a cake tin and grease it well with 1 tbsp. melted ghee. Pour in 50 ml. (5 to 6 tbsp.) of the batter. Sprinkle some cashewnuts and raisins. Bake in a hot oven till done. Remove from the oven and spread 1 tbsp. ghee all over. Pour in 50 ml. egg batter and sprinkle cashewnuts and raisins. Bake in the oven till set. Proceed thus till both the batters have been used up. On the last layer put cashewnuts and raisins lavishly. Bake till golden brown on top. Remove on to a plate and serve.

98. Chattippathiri

(Rich Chapati layer Cake)

Flour	*100 gm.*	*Sugar candy*	*2 tbsp.*
Eggs	*4*	*Ghee*	*50 ml.*
Sugar	*25 gm.*	*Milk*	*3/4 cup*
Cashewnuts	*25 gm.*	*Rose water*	*1 tsp.*
Raisins	*25 gm.*	*Cardamom powder*	*a pinch*
Poppy seeds	*2 tbsp.*		

Knead the flour with salt and water to a soft dough. Divide into 6 even-sized balls. Roll out into thin chapatis. Roll out all 6 chapatis in the same size. Heat a tava and place a chapati on it. Turn it over after a few seconds. Keep it for a second and turn it again. When both the sides are lightly cooked remove from the tava. (Be careful not to overcook.) Finish all the chapatis the same way and place them under a rolling board to prevent them from drying up. Keep aside.

Fry the cashewnuts and raisins in little ghee to a golden brown. Roast the poppy seeds without ghee. Beat eggs well with sugar and add rosewater and cardamom powder.

Take a heavy-bottomed vessel in which the chapatis should fit. Grease the vessel with melted ghee. Take one chapati and soak it in milk for a second, then dip it in the beaten egg. Put this in the vessel. Pour 3 tbsp. egg and sprinkle cashewnuts, raisins, sugar candy and poppy seed over it. Pour 2 tbsp. ghee all over. Proceed thus till all the chapatis have been used up. On the last layer pour the remaining egg and sprinkle cashewnuts, raisins, khus-khus and sugar candy lavishly. Pour the remaining ghee all over.

Put the vessel on a very low fire and cover with a lid, putting live coals on the lid. Bake it till golden brown on top. Cool and turn on to a plate.

This cake can be baked in an oven instead.

99. Palpathiri

(Egg Pudding)

Eggs	*6*	*Cashewnuts*	*50 gm.*
Milk	*250 ml.*	*Raisins*	*50 gm.*
Sugar	*150 gm.*	*Ghee*	*100 gm.*
Bengal gram dal	*100 gm.*	*Cardamom (powdered)*	*5 pods*

Beat the eggs well with sugar. Cook the dal and grind to smooth paste without adding any water. Chop the cashewnuts. Mix the ground dal with the eggs. Add the milk and beat well with an egg-beater. Add cardamom powder. Put an idli vessel with water on fire. Put in the perforated lid. Grease a small vessel with 1 tbsp. ghee and place it on the lid. Pour in 4 tbsp. egg mixture and sprinkle cashewnuts and raisins over it. Close the vessel and steam till the eggs are set. When the eggs are set apply 2 tsp. ghee and pour 4 tbsp. egg mixture. Sprinkle a little of cashewnut and raisins. Steam till set. Proceed thus till the egg mixture has been used up. Cool, cut into square or diamond-shaped pieces and serve.

100. Bariyittathu

(Banana Finger Fries)

Boiled rice	*100 gm.*	*Sugar*	*100 gm.*
Ripe bananas (yellow variety)	*6*	*Oil*	*for frying*
Egg	*1*		
Flour	*100 gm.*		

Clean and soak the boiled rice in cold water for 3 hours. Grind it smoothly to a thick paste. Mash the banana well. Add the ground rice, flour, sugar, egg and a pinch of salt. Mix well and add a little water if necessary to make a batter of dropping consistency. Heat oil. Squeeze the batter through your hands into the hot oil and fry 4-6 of these fingers in a batch to a golden brown. Remove from the oil and strain.

101. Nulliyittathu

(Sweet Egg Fritters)

Flour	*100 gm.*	*Cardamom powder*	*a pinch*
Eggs	*3*		

Semolina	*50 gm.*	*Oil*	*for frying*
Sugar	*50 gm.*	*Salt*	*to taste*

Sieve flour and add rava. Beat the egg and add sugar. Add the flour-semolina mixture, cardamom powder and a pinch of salt. Make a batter of dropping consistency. Heat the oil. Mix the batter with your hands and drop small balls of it into the hot oil. Fry to a golden brown and remove.

102. Kaiveesal

(Egg Jalebis)

Eggs	*4*	*Oil*	*for frying*
Sugar	*4 tbsp.*	*Salt*	*a pinch*
Flour (1 cup)	*100 gm.*		

Beat the eggs and sugar just enough to mix them. Add flour and make a thick batter. Add a pinch of salt. Make a small hole in a coconut shell. Heat oil in a kadai. Fill the coconut shell with batter and pour it into the hot oil like jalebis. Fry to a golden brown and remove.

103. Podippola

(Spice and Nut Cake)

Eggs	*2*	*Cardamom*	
Sugar	*50 gm.*	*(powdered)*	*3 pods*

Ghee	*1 tbsp.*	*Cashewnuts and raisins*
Flour	*50 gm.*	*for garnishing*

Beat the eggs and sugar till thick and creamy. Add the flour and mix lightly. Add the cardamom powder. Melt the ghee in a small vessel or a cake tin. Remove from the fire and pour in the egg batter. Garnish with raisins and halved cashewnuts. Bake in a hot oven till light brown on top. Remove and turn onto a plate.

104. Tharippola

(Semolina Cake)

Eggs	*2*	*Cashewnuts and raisins*
Sugar	*50 gm.*	*for garnishing*
Semolina	*100 gm.*	*Vanilla essence*
Ghee	*1 tbsp.*	*or cardamom powder*

Beat the eggs and sugar till thick and creamy. Roast semolina slightly, taking care not to brown it. Add to the eggs and mix well. Add a few drops of vanilla essence or a pinch of cardamom powder. Grease a small vessel or a cake tin with melted ghee. Pour in the egg batter. Garnish with raisins and halved cashewnuts. Bake in a hot oven till light brown on top. Remove and turn on to a plate.

Note. This can be baked keeping the vessel on a slow fire. Cover the vessel with a lid and put some live coals on top.

105. Mutta Marichathu

(Fruit and Nut Cake)

Eggs	*10*	*Raisins*	*2 tbsp.*
Sugar	*140 gm.*	*Ghee*	*1 tbsp.*
Cashewnuts (chopped)	*3 tbsp.*	*Cardamom (powdered)*	*4 pods*

Beat the eggs and sugar together till frothy. Add cardamom powder. Grease a small aluminium vessel or a cake tin with ghee. Pour in the egg mixture. Sprinkle cashewnuts and raisins. Bake in a hot oven till baked and golden brown on top.

106. Bread Porichathu

(Fried Bread Dessert)

Bread slices	*6*	*Cardamom powder*	*a pinch*
Eggs	*3*	*Ghee for shallow frying*	
Sugar	*2 tbsp.*		

Beat the eggs with sugar and add cardamom powder. Heat ghee. Dip each slice of bread in the egg mixture and put in the hot ghee. Shallow fry to a golden brown and remove.

107. Stuffed Bread

Round-loaf bread (unsliced)	*1½ lb.*	*Cashewnuts*	*3 tbsp.*
		Raisins	*2 tbsp.*

Eggs	*4*	*Cardamom (powdered)*	*4 pods*
Sugar	*100 gm.*	*Ghee*	*2 tbsp.*
Egg yolk	*1*	*Water*	
Rose water for flavouring			
Flour	*2 tsp.*		

Chop half of the cashewnuts and halve the rest. Beat four eggs with sugar. Heat the ghee. Fry the halved cashewnuts and half of the raisins to a golden brown and remove. Keep this aside for garnishing. Add eggs to the same ghee and stir continuously till scrambled and cooked. Add the chopped cashewnuts and raisins. Remove from the fire. Remove the crust from the loaf. Cut out a small round piece of bread from the bottom and keep the piece aside. Scoop out the inside without breaking the loaf.

Stuff the loaf with the scrambled egg and close the hole with the cut-out piece. Take 2 tsp. flour. Add a little water and make a paste and apply around the cut piece. Beat the egg yolk and apply this over the bread. Put the sugar in a vessel and add half cup water. Make a thin syrup. Put the bread in the syrup and pour the syrup over the bread. Turn it over and pour the syrup on. Cook till the four sides are done and the syrup is thick. Remove from the fire. Add the cardamom powder and rosewater. Remove to a shallow plate and garnish with fried cashewnuts and raisins.

108. Cashewnut Fritters

Cashewnuts	*100 gm.*	*Oil*	*for frying*

Semolina	*50 gm.*	*Vanilla essence or cardamom for flavouring*
Eggs	*2*	
Sugar	*2 tbsp.*	

Halve the cashewnuts. Beat the eggs well with sugar. Add the semolina and make a batter of dropping consistency. Add flavouring.

Heat the oil. Dip the cashewnuts in the batter and put in the hot oil. Fry to a golden brown; remove.

109. Mutta Sirka

(Rice and Egg Poories)

Boiled rice	*400 gm.*	*Oil*	*for frying*
Eggs	*4*		

Clean and soak the rice in cold water for 2-3 hours. Wash and drain the rice and grind it to a very smooth paste. beat the eggs. Add the ground rice, salt to taste and beat up well. If the batter is too thick add a little water to give it a pouring consistency. Heat oil in a kadai. Pour 1/4 cup of batter. Turn over when it puffs up. When both the sides are done remove to a colander and strain.

Note: This should be eaten with Mutta Seer or Mutton Masala.

110. Mutta Seer

(Sugared Eggs)

Sugar	*100 gm.*	*Cardamom (powdered)*	*3 pods*

Eggs	*2*	*Water*	*1 cup*

Add 1 cup water with sugar and heat till the syrup is thick. Break the eggs into the syrup. Cook till the eggs are done. Add cardamom powder and remove from the fire.

111. Pettiyappam

(Sweet Diamond Cuts in Syrup)

Flour	*500 gm.*	*Egg*	*1*
Sugar	*250 gm.*	*Oil*	*for frying*
Black cumminseed	*½ tsp.*	*Water*	
Sesame seeds	*1 tsp.*	*Salt*	

Sieve the flour. Beat the egg, add the black cumminseed and sesame seeds. Make a soft dough with flour, egg, water and salt to taste. Take small balls and roll them out thin. Cut into long strips and then cut into diamond-shaped pieces (pettiyappam). Deep fry in hot oil to golden brown and remove. Strain in a colander.

Prepare a two-string consistency syrup with the sugar and water. Put the fried *pettiyappam* in a vessel and pour the hot syrup over it. Shake the vessel to coat all the appam with syrup. Cool and store in an airtight tin.

112. Kattipettiyappam

(Sweet Fried Diamond Cuts)

Flour	*300 gm.*	*Eggs*	*3*

Semolina	*300 gm.*	*Oil*	*for frying*
Sugar	*200 gm.*		

Mix the flour and semolina together. Powder the sugar and add to this mixture. Beat the eggs. Add the eggs to the semolina mixture and knead to a thick dough. Take small portions, rolled out about 1/2 cm. thick and cut into diamond-shaped pieces. Deep fry in hot oil till light brown.

113. Kadalakkappam

(Sweet Gram Pearls)

Raw rice	*400 gm.*	*Sugar*	*500 gm.*
Bengal gram dal	*400 gm.*	*Oil*	*for frying*
Eggs	*3*		

Soak the rice and dal together for few hours. Wash and grind to a smooth paste. Add the eggs, a little salt and mix well. Heat oil. Put the ground mixture into a *boondi* ladle and press it with your hands so that drops fall into the oil. Stir the drops slightly with a spoon to avoid forming lumps. Fry to a golden brown. Remove and strain in a colander. Finish all the batter in the same way. Spread it on a thali to cool.

Make a two-string consistency syrup with sugar and water. Pour the hot syrup on to the fried *kadalakkappam*. Shake it well to coat the syrup all over. Cool and store in an airtight tin.

SAVOURY SNACKS

114. Savoury Envelope Appam

For the pancake

Maida	*1 1/2 cup*	*Milk*	*1/2 cup*
Eggs	*2*	*Salt*	*a pinch*

For the filling

Minced meat	*250 gm.*	*Coriander powder*	*1 tsp.*
Onions	*2*	*Garam masala powder*	*1/2 tsp.*
Green chillies	*4*	*Coriander leaves*	*1/2 bunch*
Ginger paste	*1 tsp.*	*Oil*	*2 tsp.*
Garlic paste	*1 tsp.*		

Cook the meat with coriander powder, turmeric powder

and salt. Chop the onion, chillies and coriander leaves. Heat the oil and add the onion and green chillies. Fry till the onion is transparent. Add the ginger and garlic paste and mutton. Fry for a while. Add the garam masala powder and coriander leaves. Remove from the fire, and keep aside. Make a thin batter with the egg, maida, milk and a little water.

Pour the batter onto a hot tava to make small pancakes about 6 cm. in diameter. Dot each one with ghee and turn over to cook on the other side. When done remove to a plate. Put a little filling in the middle of the pancake and fold the four sides to form an envelope shape. Put it in a plate. Make the second pancake bigger than the first one. When cooked remove to a plate. Put some filling in the middle of the pancake and put the first folded pancake on the filling. Now fold the four edges as for the first one. Seal the edges with a little batter. Keep it on the tava with sealed edges down and press it a little to make it firm. Remove from tava. Make a third pancake bigger than the second and proceed as before. Make two more envelope appams with the remaining batter and filling.

Note. The appams can be made bigger if you make four or five layers instead of three.

115. Thurkkippathil

(Stuffed Mutton Pie)

Minced mutton	*200 gm.*	*Ginger paste*	*1 tsp.*
Onions (big)	*2*	*Garlic paste*	*1 tsp.*
Green chillies	*4*	*Garam masala powder*	*½ tsp.*
Coriander powder	*1 tsp.*	*Coriander leaves*	*½ bunch*
Chilli powder	*¼ tsp.*	*Oil*	*1 tbsp.*

Turmeric powder	*1/4 tsp.*	*Salt*	*to taste*

For covering

Flour	*300 gm.*	*Water*	
Salt	*`to taste*		

Egg filling

Eggs	*4*	*Cashewnuts (chopped)*	*2 tbsp.*
Sugar	*2 tbsp.*	*Raisins*	*2 tbsp.*
Ghee	*2 tsp.*	*Cardamom (powdered)*	*4 pods*

Knead the flour to a soft dough with salt and water. Keep aside.

Mutton filling
Cook the mince with coriander powder, turmeric powder, chilli powder and salt, till the mutton is soft and the water is absorbed. Chop onion, chillies and coriander leaves.

Heat the oil. Add the onion and green chillies. Fry till the onion is lightly browned. Add the ginger and garlic paste and fry for a while. Add the mutton and fry for a few seconds more. Add the garam masala powder and coriander leaves. Remove from the fire.

Egg filling
Beat the eggs with sugar. Heat the ghee and add egg. Stir well till scrambled and the eggs are cooked. Add the cashewnuts, raisins and cardamom powder. Remove from the fire.

Take a small ball of dough, roll it out and cut it into 2

rounds of 6 cm. diameter. Fry them in oil like puris. Put a little egg filling on one puri and cover it with the other puri. Now make a second puri bigger than the first (about 12 cm. diameter). Before frying, put some mutton filling in the centre. Place the filled-up puri on top of the mutton filling and cover it nicely to form the shape of a pumpkin. Pinch off the extra dough from the top. Fry it in oil to a golden brown and remove. Now make a third chapati bigger than the second. Put some egg filling in the centre and place the fried pumpkin-shaped ball on top of the filling. Cover it up as before and shape it like a pumpkin. Fry it in hot oil to golden brown.

Note. This can be made bigger by making one or two layers more.

116. Irachi Pathiri

(Stuffed Mutton Puris)

Wholewheat flour	*400 gm.*	*Cashewnuts*	*1 tbsp.*
Minced mutton	*200 gm.*	*Turmeric powder*	*½ tbsp.*
Onions	*2*	*Garam masala powder*	*1 tsp.*
Green chillies	*4*	*Aniseed*	*1 tsp.*
Ginger	*2 cm. piece*	*Garlic*	*4 cloves*
Coriander powder	*2 tsp.*	*Hardboiled egg*	*1*
Coriander leaves	*½ bunch*	*Oil*	*for frying*
Raisins	*1 tbsp.*	*Salt*	*to taste*

Make a soft dough with the flour and salted water and keep aside. Cook the minced mutton with coriander powder, turmeric powder, ground aniseed and salt, till the meat is tender and water is absorbed. Slice the onion fine. Chop the green chillies and coriander leaves. Grind the garlic and ginger. Chop the cashewnuts. Clean and wash the raisins.

Heat 1 tbsp. oil and fry the onions till transparent. Add chillies, ginger and garlic paste, and stir. Add mutton, cashewnuts, raisins and coriander leaves. Sprinkle garam masala powder. Stir well and remove from fire.

Divide the dough into 8 balls. Cut the hardboiled egg into eight pieces. Divide the mutton into four portions. Roll out each ball of dough into chapati-like round 8 cm. in diameter. Take one portion of meat mixture and spread it evenly on one 'chapati'. Place 2 pieces of egg in the middle and cover with another 'chapati'. Press the edges well and then cut them with a cutter.

Deep fry in hot oil, till golden brown.

117. Athishaya Pathiri
(Pancake Bake)

For stuffing

Minced mutton	*250 gm.*	*Garam masala powder*	*1 tsp.*
Onions (big)	*2*	*Coriander leaves*	*½ bunch*
Green chillies	*4*	*Raisins*	*2 tbsp.*
Garlic	*½ pod*	*Cashewnuts (chopped)*	*2 tbsp.*
Ginger	*1 cm. piece*	*Ghee*	*3 tbsp.*
Coriander powder	*1 tsp.*	*Salt*	*to taste*
Turmeric powder	*½ tsp.*		

For pancake

Flour	*150 gm.*	*Ghee*	*2 tbsp.*
Eggs	*2*	*Salt*	*to taste*
Milk or coconut milk	*1 cup*		

For egg mixture

Eggs	*4*	*Beat eggs well and add*

Green Chillies	*2*	*ground green*
Salt	*to taste*	*chillies and salt*

Cook the meat with coriander powder, turmeric powder and salt till it is tender and the water is absorbed. Chop the onions, green chillies and coriander leaves. Grind the garlic and ginger. Heat 1 tbsp. ghee and saute onion and chillies. Fry till the onion is transparent. Add the ginger and garlic paste. Stir for a while. Add the cooked mince and cook till dry. Add the coriander leaves, garam masala powder, cashewnuts and raisins (reserving some cashewnuts and raisins for garnishing). Keep aside.

For pancake

Make a thin batter with the flour, eggs, milk and salt. If the milk is not sufficient add a little water. Heat a frying pan and pour in 2 tbsp. of the batter and turn the pan in a circular way to form a thin pancake. Apply a little ghee and when it is cooked turn it over. When the other side is also cooked, remove. Finish all the batter the same way. Keep aside.

Grease a heavy-bottomed small vessel or a cake tin (in which the pancake fits) with 3 tsp. ghee. Take a pancake and dip it well in the egg mixture. Put it in the vessel and place a layer of minced meat over it. Cover this layer with another pancake dipped in egg mixture and proceed thus till all the pancakes have been used. On the top layer pour the remaining egg and garnish with cashewnuts and raisins. Dot with one tablespoon ghee. Place the vessel on a slow fire covering it with a heavy tight-fitting lid. Place some coals on top and keep for about 20 minutes till it is cooked and golden brown on top. Remove to a plate and serve.

Note. This can be baked in an oven.

118. Koyiada

(Mutton Samosa)

Minced mutton	*200 gm.*	*Coriander powder*	*1 tsp.*
Flour	*100 gm.*	*Turmeric powder*	*1/4 tsp.*
Onion (big)	*1*	*Garam masala powder*	*1/4 tsp.*
Green chillies	*4*	*Coriander leaves*	*1/2 bunch*
Ginger paste	*1/2 tsp.*	*Oil*	*for frying*
Garlic paste	*1/2 tsp.*		

Cook the mutton with coriander powder, turmeric powder and salt, till the mutton is done and the water is absorbed. Chop the onion, green chillies and coriander leaves. Heat 2 tsp. oil. Add the onion and chillies. Fry till the onion is lightly brown. Add the ginger and garlic paste, mutton, coriander leaves and garam masala. Fry for a few seconds more. Remove from the fire and keep aside. Make a smooth dough with the flour, salt and water. Take a small ball and roll it out thinly. Cut it out with a small round cutter. Place some meat filling on one side and fold the other half over to form a semi-circle. Press the edges well and pinch with fingers or cut the edges with a cutter. Heat the oil and deep fry the Koyiadas to a golden brown and remove.

119. Bajiya

Thoor dal	*1 cup*	*Garlic*	*5 flakes*
Onion (big)	*1*	*Coriander leaves*	*1/2 bunch*
Green chillies	*4*	*Curry leaves*	*few sprigs*
Chilli powder	*1/2 tsp.*	*Oil*	*for frying*
Turmeric powder	*1/4 tsp.*	*Salt*	*to taste*

Wash and soak the dal for an hour and grind coarsely. Chop the onion, green chillies, coriander leaves and curry leaves. Crush the garlic. Add all the ingredients to the dal and mix it well. Add salt to taste. Heat the oil. Shape the mixture into vadas, deep fry to a golden brown and remove.

120. Stuffed Bread

Round-loaf bread (unsliced)	*1½ lb.*	*Garlic paste*	*1 tsp.*
Minced mutton	*200 gm.*	*Coriander powder*	*2 tsp.*
Hardboiled egg	*1*	*Garam masala powder*	*1 tsp.*
Egg, beaten	*1*	*Turmeric powder*	*½ tsp.*
Onions (big)	*2*	*Cashewnuts (chopped)*	*1 tbsp.*
Green chillies	*4*	*Raisins*	*1 tsp.*
Ginger paste	*1 tsp.*	*Oil*	*1 tbsp.*

Cook the minced mutton with coriander powder, turmeric powder and salt with sufficient water till the mutton is soft and the water is absorbed. Chop the onion, chillies and coriander leaves. Heat the oil and saute the onion and chillies. Add the ginger and garlic paste and fry till the aroma comes. Add the minced mutton and fry till it is dry. Add the cashewnuts, raisins, coriander leaves and garam masala powder. Remove from the fire. Keep it aside.

Remove the crust from the bread. Cut out a small round piece of bread from the bottom and keep the piece aside. Carefully scoop out the inside. Add a little of the scooped bread to the mince. Stuff the bread with mince and whole hardboiled egg. Close the hole with the cut-out piece. Smear the bread with the beaten egg. Heat 4 tbsp. oil in a frying pan and shallow-fry the bread.

121. Kuzahalappam

(Rice Curls)

Raw rice	*400 gm.*	*Black cumminseed*	*2 tsp.*
Coconut	*½*	*Oil*	*for frying*

Pick and soak the rice in water for 2-3 hours. Wash and drain till dry. Powder and sieve through a fine sieve. Roast the flour and cool it. Extract 2 cups coconut milk. Heat the coconut milk. Add salt, rice flour and black cumminseed. Stir well till the flour is mixed. Remove from the fire and cool. Knead to form a fairly stiff dough. Divide into small balls. Roll out to rounds of about 4 cm. diameter. Shape round your fingers to form tubes. Deep fry in hot oil till crisp. Strain in a colander and cool.

122. Chukkappam

(Rice Buttons)

Rice flour	*400 gm.*	*Black cumminseed*	*2 tsp.*
Eggs	*2*	*Ghee*	*2 tbsp.*
Water	*2 cups*	*Chopped onion (small)*	*2 tsp.*

Heat ghee in a vessel and add the chopped onion. When the onion turns light brown pour water, add salt and cover. When the water boils add the flour, make a hole in the centre of the flour and cover the vessel. Keep on a low fire for few seconds. Uncover, stir well and remove from the fire and cool. Beat the eggs very lightly. Add black cumminseed. Knead the flour to a smooth dough by adding the egg batter little by little. Take a little of the dough and roll it out like a pencil. From these rolls take small balls, roll each and press it to form little buttons. Deep fry in hot oil to golden brown. Remove and strain in colander. When cold add to Fried Mutton.

123. Fried Mutton

Mutton without bones	*250 gm.*	*Turmeric powder*	*½ tsp.*
Chilli powder	*½ tsp.*	*Aniseed*	*1 tsp.*
Coriander powder	*2 tsp.*	*Oil*	*for frying*

Cut the mutton into 4 cm. pieces and wash. Grind aniseed. Cook the mutton with all the ingredients, water and salt to taste, till the mutton is soft and water is absorbed. Heat the oil and deep-fry the mutton till crisp. Remove and strain. Add to the chukkappam and mix. Store in air-tight tins.

PICKLES AND CHUTNEYS

124. Date Pickle

Dates	*250 gm.*	*Garlic*	*100 gm.*
Red chillies	*25 gm.*	*Salt*	*25 gm.*
Ginger	*100 gm.*	*Vinegar*	
		(3/4 bottle)	*500 ml.*

Wash the dates and dry with a cloth. Stone and cut into halves. Wash, peel and cut the ginger into long pieces. Peel the garlic. Dry the chillies in the sun and powder.

Put all the ingredients except chilli powder in a jar. Keep it aside for two days. Add chilli powder and stir well and keep aside. The pickle is ready after two days.

125. Papaya Pickle

Small raw papaya (about ½ kg.)	*1*	*Garlic*	*150 gm.*
Red chillies	*25 gm.*	*Vinegar*	*500 ml.*
Ginger	*150 gm.*	*Salt*	*30 gm.*

Wash, peel and slice the papaya and ginger into thin pieces 3 cm. long. Peel the garlic. Put the papaya, ginger and garlic in a jar. Add vinegar and salt. Keep it aside for two days. Dry the chillies in the sun and powder. Add to the pieces. Mix well and keep it aside for two days more before using.

126. Date And Lime Pickle

Limes	*10*	*Red chillies*	*25 gm.*
Dates	*200 gm.*	*Vinegar*	*750 ml.*
Ginger	*50 gm.*		
Garlic	*2 pods*		

Wash the limes and wipe them. Cut each into eight pieces. Wash and dry the dates. Stone and cut into two. Wash and peel the ginger and cut it into 2 cm. long pieces. Peel the garlic. Dry the chillies in the sun and powder.

N.P. Put the lime pieces and salt in a jar and keep for three days. On the fourth day add all the ingredients except chilli powder. Add chilli powder the next day and keep for one or two days more. The pickle is ready within a week.

127. Carrot Pickle

Carrots	*250 gm.*	*Ginger*	*100 gm.*
Garlic	*100 gm.*	*Red chillies*	*25 gm.*
Vinegar	*½ bottle*	*Salt*	*30 gm.*

Wash, peel and cut the carrots and ginger into 3 cm.-long strips. Spread out on a piece of cloth and dry well. Peel the garlic. Dry the chillies in the sun and powder. Put all the ingredients except the chilli powder into a jar and keep aside for two days. Add the chilli powder, stir well and keep for two days more and use.

128. Bitter Gourd Pickle

Ginger	*50 gm.*	*Mustard seeds*	*1 tsp.*
Garlic	*50 gm.*	*Curry leaves*	
Vinegar	*300 ml.*	*Salt*	*to taste*
Gingelly oil or OK oil	*150 ml.*	*Small onions*	*100 gm.*
Sugar	*2 tbsp.*	*Green chillies*	*50 gm.*
Bitter gourd	*250 gm.*		

Wash and cut the bitter gourd into round slices. Peel and slice the onion, garlic and ginger into long pieces. Slit the green chillies. Heat the oil. Add mustard; when it starts to crackle add the bitter gourd, onion, chillies, ginger, garlic and curry leaves. Fry for about five minutes till the bitter gourd turns transparent. Add the vinegar and salt. Stir well and keep on fire till the bitter gourd is cooked. Add the sugar and remove from the fire. Cool and bottle

129. Uppunaranga

Limes	*25*	*Salt*	*200 gm.*
Black cumminseed	*1 tsp.*	*Vinegar*	*300 ml.*

Wash the limes. Boil water in a pan. When water boils put in the limes. Keep on the fire for a minute without covering. Remove from the fire and strain in a colander. When cool, wipe with a cloth. Slit each lime into four halfway down. Mix the salt and black cumminseed together and stuff limes with this. Pack into a clean dry jar. Sprinkle the excess salt in the jar. Cover and keep for a week. Shake the jar everyday. When all the salt is dissolved add vinegar. The limes should be covered with vinegar. Keep for two weeks before using.

Note. This pickle can be kept for one year.

130. Uppu Manga

Matured mangoes (medium-size)	*25*	*Water*	*2 lit.*
Salt	*200 gm.*		

Boil water in a large pan. Add the washed mangoes and keep uncovered for five minutes or till the mango turns pale in colour. Remove from the fire and strain in a colander. Spread onto a clean mat or cloth and keep till completely cool.

Dissolve the salt in the water and strain through a

muslin cloth. Pack the mangoes in a clean dry jar and cover with salt water. Cover the jar and tie a piece of cloth over it. Keep till the mangoes become soft. Cut into pieces before serving. Serve with green chillies or red chillies roasted on live coals.

Note. This pickle can be kept for six months.

131. Coconut Chutney

Coconut	*½*	*Curry leaves*	*1 sprig*
Green chillies	*6*	*Vinegar or juice of ½ lime*	*2 tsp.*
Ginger	*2 cm. piece*	*Salt*	*to taste*
Coriander leaves	*½ bunch*		

Grate the coconut. Grind the chillies, coriander leaves curry leaves and salt. Add the coconut and grind it together to a smooth paste. Add vinegar or lime juice.

132. Coconut Mango Chutney

Coconut	*½*	*Garlic*	*2 cloves*
Raw mango (small)	*1*	*Salt*	*to taste*
Red chillies	*6*		

Grate the coconut. Grind the chillies, mango and salt. Add the coconut and grind coarsely. Add the garlic and grind all together and remove.

133. Massu Chutney

(Maldive Fish Chutney)

Coconut (grated)	*½*	*Onion (big)*	*1*
Red chillies	*6*	*Juice of ½ lime*	
Pounded maldive fish (dried tuna)	*½ cup*	*Salt*	*to taste*

Grind the chillies and salt. Add the coconut and grind together. Add the maldive fish, grind coarsely and mix together and remove. Chop the onion fine and add to the chutney. Add the lime juice and mix well.

134. Mango Chutney

Raw mango	*1*	*Garlic*	*2 cloves*
Red chillies	*5*	*Salt*	*to taste*

Peel and slice the mango. Grind all the ingredients together.

135. Curd Chutney

Coconut	*½*	*Curd*	*½ cup*
Red chillies	*6*	*Salt*	*to taste*
Garlic	*3 cloves*		

Grate the coconut. Grind the chillies and salt. Add the coconut and garlic. Grind to a smooth paste. Beat the curd and mix with the chutney.

136. Chakkara Puli

(Sweet Tamarind)

Tamarind	*100 gm.*	*Oil*	*3 tsp.*
Jaggery	*150 gm.*	*Mustard seeds*	*1 pinch*
Red chillies	*10*	*Salt*	*to taste*
Garlic	*6 cloves*		

Soak the tamarind in a little water and take out the pulp. Grind the chillies, garlic and salt. Grate the jaggery. Add the jaggery and tamarind pulp to the ground chillies.

Heat the oil. Add mustard and when it crackles add the chutney. Boil and remove from the fire.

Note. This can be kept for a week.

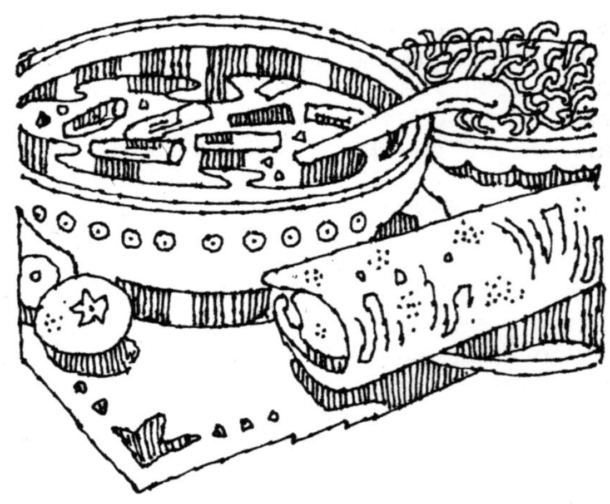

137. Macaroni Mutton

Cut Macaroni	*200 gm.*	*Chilli powder*	*1 tsp.*
Mutton	*250 gm.*	*Turmeric powder*	*1/2 tsp.*
Onions (big)	*2*	*Aniseed*	*1 tsp.*
Green chillies	*6*	*Cinnamon*	*4 cm. piece*
Garlic	*1 pod*	*Cloves*	*4*
Ginger	*4 cm. piece*	*Cardamom*	*3 pods*
Coconut	*1/2*	*Coriander leaves*	*1/2 bunch*
Coriander powder	*2 tbsp.*	*Oil*	*50 ml.*

Cut the mutton into small pieces and wash. Cook the mutton with coriander powder, chilli powder, turmeric powder and salt till soft. Grind the ginger and garlic to a paste. Grind the coconut with aniseed, cloves, cinnamon and cardamom to a fine paste. Slice the onion and chillies. Chop coriander leaves. Cook the macaroni in salt water till soft. Strain in a colander and rinse in cold water.

Heat the oil and saute onion and green chillies. Add ginger and garlic paste and fry for a few minutes. Add the cooked meat and stir well. Simmer for a few minutes. Mix the ground coconut in a cup of water and add to the meat. Cook for a few minutes more. Add the macaroni and stir. Cook for a few minutes on a slow fire. Add the chopped coriander leaves and remove from fire.

138. Drumstick Soup

Drumstick leaves	*1 bunch*	*Butter or margarine*	*1 tbsp.*
Onion (big)	*1*	*Milk*	*1 cup*
Flour	*1 tbsp.*	*Tomato sauce*	*4 tbsp.*
Tomatoes	*200 gm.*	*Stock or water*	*4 cups*

Pick and wash the drumstick leaves. Take all the tender stems and chop. Chop tomatoes and onions.

Cook the drumstick leaves and stems with the tomatoes and onions in 4 cups stock or water till the leaves are tender. Reserving a handful of leaves for garnishing, strain the cooked vegetables through a sieve to make a puree. Prepare a white sauce with flour, butter and milk. Add the vegetable puree. Season with salt and pepper. Add the drumstick leaves and simmer for 5 minutes. Remove from the fire. Add the tomato sauce and serve hot.

139. Bread Kofta Curry

For the Koftas

Leftover bread	*6 slices*
Minced mutton or leftover cooked mutton	*100 gm.*
Coriander leaves	*½ bunch*
Onion (big)	*1*
Green chillies	*8*
Ginger	*2 cm. piece*
Oil	*for frying*
Garam masala powder	*¼ tsp.*
Lime juice	*few drops*
Salt	*to taste*

For the gravy

Onion (big)	*1*
Tomatoes (big)	*2*
Garlic	*4 cloves*
Ginger	*2 cm. piece*
Green chillies	*2*
Coriander powder	*2 tsp.*
Chilli powder	*½ tsp.*
Turmeric powder	*½ tsp.*
Garam masala powder	*½ tsp.*
Coriander leaves	*½ bunch*
Curd	*½ cup*
Juice of lime	*½*
Oil	*3 tbsp.*
Water	*1 cup*

Cook the mutton in a little water with salt till the water is absorbed. Chop onions, green chillies, ginger and coriander leaves.

Heat 2 tsp. oil. Saute onions, green chillies and ginger. When the onions are done add meat. Stir for a while. Add coriander leaves and remove from the fire. Sprinkle lime juice and garam masala powder and keep aside. Cut the crust from the bread. Soak the bread in water and squeeze out the water. Knead into a soft dough. Divide the dough into 6 small balls. Divide the mince also into 6 portions. Take one ball and form into a cup shape. Fill up the cup with one portion of mince, close it to form a ball. Make five more koftas thus. Heat oil and fry them golden brown and keep aside.

To make the gravy, grind onion, green chillies, ginger and garlic separately. Grind the coriander powder, chilli powder and turmeric powder together to a smooth paste. Blanch the tomatoes and make a puree. Beat the curd. Heat oil. Add the ground onion, garlic, ginger and green chilli paste and fry for few seconds. Add the other ground ingredients and fry for few seconds more. Add tomato puree, salt, curd and one cup water. Simmer for a few seconds. Add the coriander leaves and garam masala powder. Remove from the fire. Place the fried koftas in a serving dish and pour the curry over them. Sprinkle over with lime juice and serve immediately.

140. Vermicelli and Egg

Vermicelli	*100 gm.*
Eggs	*3*
Onion (big)	*1*
Green chillies	*4*
Ginger	*2 cm. piece*
Garlic	*4 cloves*
Coriander powder	*2 tsp.*
Garam masala powder	*½ tsp*
Cashewnuts (chopped)	*1 tbsp.*
Raisins	*1 tbsp.*
Coriander leaves	*½ bunch*
Ghee or oil	*4 tbsp.*
Lime juice	*1 tsp.*
a little yellow colouring powder	

Slice the onion fine. Chop the coriander leaves. Grind ginger, garlic and green chillies. Hard-boil one egg and beat the other two eggs. Heat 2 tbsp. ghee. Fry the cashewnuts and raisins and remove. Add onion and fry till lightly browned. Add the ground masala and fry for a while. Add coriander powder and stir well. Add beaten eggs and stir well till the eggs are done.

Remove from the fire.

Heat the remaining ghee in a separate vessel and fry the vermicelli till lightly browned. Add one cup water and salt to taste. Cook till the vermicelli is done and the water is absorbed. Add the colouring powder mixed in a little water. Add the egg masala, lime juice, coriander leaves and garam masala powder. Stir well and remove from the fire. Arrange in a serving dish and garnish with sliced hard-boiled eggs, fried cashewnuts and raisins.

141. Dosa Dahi Vada

Left-over dosas	*6*	*Curry leaves*	*1 sprig*
Grated coconut	*1 cup*	*Curd*	*1 cup*
Coriander leaves	*½ bunch*	*Salt*	*to taste*
Green chillies	*2*		

Grind the coconut with chillies, coriander leaves, curry leaves and salt to taste. Beat the curd and add to the chutney. Place one dosa in a plate and pour 2 tbsp. chutney on it. Spread it evenly on the dosa. Place another dosa on the chutney. Pour 2 tbsp. chutney and spread it evenly. Make one more dosa and chutney layer. Carefully roll it up without breaking. Cut into 2 cm. slices. Use up all the dosa this way.

Garnish with chilli powder and coriander leaves.

142. Liver Baji

Liver cooked with a little turmeric and salt (or leftover liver)	*200 gm.*	*Chilli powder*	*1 tsp.*
Gram flour	*100 gm.*	*Oil*	*for frying*
		Baking powder	*a pinch*

Cut the liver into small pieces. Make a thick batter with gram flour, chilli powder, baking powder and salt. Dip each piece of liver in the batter and deep-fry in hot oil.

143. Mutta Paratha

Leftover parathas	*4*	*Green chillies*	*2*
Eggs	*4*	*Ghee*	*4 tbsp.*
Onion (big)	*1*	*Pepper and salt to taste*	

Cut the parathas into small pieces. Grind the onion and chillies. Beat the eggs and add ground onion, chillies, salt and pepper. Add the paratha pieces and mix well. Heat the ghee in a frying pan. Put in the paratha-egg mixture and stir well. When the eggs are done remove from the fire.

GLOSSARY

ENGLISH	MALAYALAM	HINDI
Aniseed	Perunjeerakam	Saunf
Almond	Badam	Badam
Arrow-root	Koova	Arrow-root
Asafoetida	Kayam	Heeng
Banana	Neenthrapazham	Kela
Beans	Payary	Sem
Bitter gourd	Kayippakka/ Pavakka	Karela
Black cumminseed	Karinjeerakam	Kala jeera
Bread	Rotti	Double Roti
Butter	Veena	Makhan
Bengal gram dal	Kadala Parippu	Channa dal
Black gram dal	Uzhunnu Parippu	Urad dal
Boiled rice	Puzhungalari	Sela chaval/ Usnachaval
Brinjal	Vazhuthininga	Baingan
Beaten rice	Avil	Chivda, Poha
Cabbage	Muttakose	Band Gobi
Cardamom	Elathari	Ilaichi
Carrot	Mullanki/Carrot	Gajar
Cashewnuts	Andi Parippu	Kajoo
Cakeseed	Sajeerakam	Shahjeera
Chicken	Kozhi	Murgi
Chillies (red)	Chukanna Mulaku	Lal Mirch

ENGLISH	MALAYALAM	HINDI
Chillies (green)	Pacha Mulaku	Hari Mirch
Cinnamon	Karuvopatta	Dalchini
Cloves	Karyambu	Laung
Coconut	Thenga	Nariyal
Coriander seed	Kothambalari/ Kothamalli	Dhania
Coriander leaves	Malli ela	Hara Dhania
Cream	Pal pada	Malai
Cumin	Nalla Jeerakam	Jeera
Curd	Thayir	Dahi
Curry leaves	Karuveppila	Kari Patta (Meetha neem ka patta)
Dal (Lentils)	Parippu	Dal
Dates	Eethapazham	Khajur
Drumstick	Muringakkai	Sehjan
Drumstick leaves	Murunga Ila	Sehjan ki patti
Egg	Mutta	Anda
Fenugreek	Uluva	Methi
Fish	Meen	Machli
Figs	Athipazham	Anjeer
Flour: Gram	Khadalapodi	Besan, chane ka atta
Refined	Maida	Maida
Wholemeal (wheat)	Godamba Podi	Atta, Gehu ka atta
Garlic	Veluthulli	Lehsan
Ginger	Inchi	Adrak
Green gram	Cherupayar	Moong dal
Gooseberry	Nellikka	Amla
Honey	Theyn	Shahad
Jackfruit	Chakka	Katahal

ENGLISH	MALAYALAM	HINDI
Jaggery	Vellam	Gud
Ladies' finger (okra)	Vendekka	Bhindi
Lime	Cherunaranga	Nimbu
Liver	Karal	Kaleji
Mace	Jathipathri	Jaithri
Mango (raw)	Manga	Kacha Am
Mint leaves	Pudeena	Pudina
Milk	Pal	Doodh
Mustard	Kaduku	Sarson
Mutton	Erachi	Gosht
Minced mutton	Keema	Keema
Nutmeg	Jathikka	Jaiphal
Oil	Enna	Tel
Onion	Ulli	Pyaz
Orange	Mathuranaranga	Naranhi/ Santra
Papaya	Karamoosa	Papita
Peas	Pattani	Matar
Pepper	Kurumullaku	Kali mirch
Poppy seed	Vella khus khus	Khus khus
Potato	Urulakizhangu	Alu
Pineapple	Kaithachakka	Ananas
Raisins	Munthiringa	Kish mish
Rice	Ari	Chaval
Rose water	Pananeer	Ghulab Jal
Saffron	Kumkumam	Zafran/Kesar
Salt	Uppu	Namak
Semolina	Rava/Thari	Sooji
Sesame seed	Ellu	Til
Sugar	Panchasara	Chinni/ Shakkar
Sugar candy	Kalkandam	Mishri
Tamarind	Puli	Imli

ENGLISH	MALAYALAM	HINDI
Tomato	Thakkali	Tamatar
Turmeric	Manjal	Haldi
Vermicelli	Semia	Semia
Vinegar	Sirka	Sirka
Wheat	Gothambam	Gehu
Walnut	Akhrot	Aḳhrot
Yam	Chena	Sooran/ Zaminkand
Fish varieties		
Crab	Nhandu	Kekda
Cat fish	Etta	Ashalk machli
Lobster	Aanakonchan	Bada Jheenga
Mackerel	Aila	Bangda
Mullet	Thirutha	Malina
Prawn	Chemmeen/ Konjan	Jheenga
Pomfret	Avoli/Akoli	Chamna
Oyster	Muru	Ghongha
Sardine	Mathi	Hari machli
Seer fish	Ayakora	
Shark	Sravu	Shark/Hangar
Silver bellies	Mullan	Rajat

INDEX OF RECIPES AND MAIN INGREDIENTS

Both recipes and main ingredients are listed here. Recipes are also listed under the main ingredients which are used in them. Recipes appear in bold type, thus:

Mutton Pulao 8
The main ingredients are given in Roman type, thus:
Banana
and the recipes listed under them are in italics, thus:
Banana in Syrup, 87

The numbers refer to recipe numbers, not to page numbers